LA CUCINA DELLA HOUSEWIFE'S MEDITERRANEAN DIET COOKBOOK

TALES AND RECIPES FROM AN ITALIAN GRANDMOTHER'S KITCHEN

Table of Contents

Introduction — 7
Pasta — 8
1. Spaghetti with Fresh Tomato Sauce — 8
2. Linguine with Clam Sauce — 9
3. Pasta alla Norma — 10
4. Penne alla Vodka — 11
5. Fettuccine Alfredo — 12
6. Spaghetti with Meatballs — 13
7. Pesto Pasta — 14
8. Orecchiette with Broccoli Rabe and Sausage — 15
9. Stuffed Shells — 16
10. Pasta with Sun-Dried Tomato and Olive Pesto — 17

Soups — 18
11. Lentil Soup with Kale and Carrots — 18
12. Minestrone Soup with Tomatoes, Zucchini, and Beans — 19
13. Tomato and Basil Soup with Croutons — 20
14. Chickpea and Spinach Soup with Lemon — 21
15. Roasted Red Pepper Soup with Feta and Herbs — 22
16. Carrot and Ginger Soup with a Hint of Harissa — 23
17. Chicken and Rice Soup with Lemon and Oregano — 24
18. Fish Soup with Clams, Mussels, and Shrimp — 25
19. Broccoli and Stilton Soup with a Drizzle of Olive Oil — 26
20. Gazpacho with Cucumber, Red Bell Pepper, and Breadcrumbs — 27

Salads — 28
21. Grilled Eggplant and Tomato Salad — 28
22. Greek Salad with Cucumber, Tomato, and Feta — 29
23. Tabbouleh with Parsley, Mint, and Bulgur Wheat — 30
24. Caprese Salad with Fresh Mozzarella and Basil — 31
25. Mediterranean Chickpea Salad with Red Onion and Feta — 32
26. Mediterranean Roasted Vegetable Salad with Balsamic Dressing — 33
27. Marinated Vegetable Salad with Artichokes, Peppers, and Olives — 34
28. Lebanese Lentil Salad with Cilantro and Lemon — 35
29. Farro Salad with Arugula, Cherry Tomatoes, and Feta — 36
30. Mediterranean Quinoa Salad with Roasted Red Pepper and Kalamata Olives — 37

Meat — 38
31. Grilled Lamb Chops with Rosemary and Garlic — 38
32. Slow-Cooked Beef Shanks with Red Wine and Thyme — 39
33. Rack of Pork with a Honey and Mustard Glaze — 40
34. Lovely Pork Medallions — 41
35. Stuffed Bell Peppers with Ground Beef and Rice — 42
36. Braised Beef Short Ribs with Carrots and Parsnips — 43
37. Beef Kofta Skewers with Yogurt and Cucumber Sauce — 44
38. Grilled Flank Steak with Chimichurri Sauce — 45
39. Slow-Cooked Bolognese Sauce with Ground Beef and Tomatoes — 46
40. Mediterranean Beef and Bulgur Wheat Salad with Herbs and Feta — 47

Poultry — 48
41. Grilled Turkey Kebabs — 48
42. Chicken Shawarma with Tabbouleh — 49

43. Mediterranean Roasted Chicken	50
44. Chicken Tagine with Apricots and Almonds	51
45. Lemon and Herb Stuffed Turkey Breast	52
46. Chicken Souvlaki	53
47. Mediterranean Chicken Salad	54
48. Chicken and Olive Tapenade	55
49. Chicken and Mushroom Risotto	56
50. Moroccan Chicken with Preserved Lemons	57

Seafood — 58

51. Grilled Mediterranean Sea Bass with Olive Tapenade and Lemon	58
52. Salmon with Roasted Red Pepper Sauce and Herbed Quinoa	59
53. Stuffed Clams with Breadcrumbs, Parsley, and Lemon	60
54. Shrimp Skewers with Charred Tomato and Basil Salsa	61
55. Seared Scallops with Tomato, Caper, and Olive Relish	62
56. Baked Cod with Tomatoes, Olives, and Feta Cheese	63
57. Grilled Octopus with Potato, Lemon, and Parsley Salad	64
58. Squid Ink Risotto with Shrimp, Tomatoes, and Parsley	65
59. Air Fryer Beef and Truffle Fries	66
60. Grilled Tuna Steak with Cucumber, Mint, and Lemon Salad	67

Vegetables — 68

61. Ratatouille	68
62. Roasted Cauliflower Steaks with Chimichurri	69
63. Roasted Red Pepper and Feta Stuffed Portobello Mushrooms	70
64. Grilled Asparagus with Lemon and Parmesan	71
65. Mediterranean Stuffed Bell Peppers	72
66. Pan-Fried Zucchini and Squash with Mint and Feta	73
67. Eggplant Parmesan	74
68. Grilled Artichokes with Lemon and Garlic	74
69. Caramelized Onion, Tomato, and Feta Tart	76
70. Roasted Carrot and Chickpea Salad with Tahini Dressing	77

Side Dishes — 78

71. Roasted Eggplant with Feta and Mint	78
72. Grilled Zucchini and Yellow Squash with Herbs	79
73. Ratatouille with Tomatoes, Bell Peppers, and Eggplant	80
74. Stuffed Artichokes with Lemon and Garlic	81
75. Grilled Portobello Mushrooms with Balsamic Glaze	82
76. Sweet Potato Fries with Rosemary and Sea Salt	83
77. Mediterranean-style Grilled Asparagus with Lemon and Parmesan	84
78. Roasted Cauliflower with Tahini and Paprika	85
79. Israeli Couscous Salad with Chickpeas, Tomatoes, and Herbs	86
80. Quinoa and Roasted Vegetable Salad with Feta and Lemon Dressing	87

Appetizers — 88

81. Stuffed Grape Leaves (Dolmades)	88
82. Grilled Eggplant Rolls with Feta and Mint	89
83. Roasted Red Pepper and Feta Dip	90
84. Marinated Olives and Feta	91
85. Fried Zucchini with Yogurt Dip	92
86. Spinach and Feta Puffs (Spanakopita)	93
87. Fried Artichokes with Lemon Aioli	94
88. Baked Feta with Honey and Thyme	95
89. Roasted Eggplant and Tomato Bruschetta	96
90. Marinated Mushrooms with Herbs and Garlic	97
91. Greek Yogurt with Honey and Walnuts	98

92. Baklava 99
93. Rosewater and Pistachio Panna Cotta 100
94. Orange and Almond Olive Oil Cake 101
95. Figs and Honey Tart 102
96. Almond and Lemon Semolina Cake 103
97. Date and Walnut Baklava Rolls 104
98. Chilled Honeydew and Mint Soup 105
99. Cinnamon Roasted Apples 106
100. Cinnamon Roasted Apples 107

Conclusion **109**

Introduction

Hello there, my name is Maria and I am a lover of food and all things Mediterranean. I've always been fascinated with the Mediterranean diet and the way it has been incorporated into the lifestyle of the people living in that region. The way they use herbs, spices, and olive oil to enhance the flavor of their dishes is just magical! So, I decided to take a leap of faith and move to the beautiful coast of the Mediterranean to learn the secrets of the cuisine and immerse myself in the local culture. And boy, was it worth it! The fresh ingredients, the vibrant colors, and the rich flavors have completely changed my outlook on food and cooking. I've had the privilege to learn from local grandmothers and chefs who have been cooking for generations, and now I want to share my newfound knowledge with you. This cookbook is a compilation of 100 of my favorite Mediterranean-style recipes, including 10 pasta dishes, 10 soups, 10 salads, 10 meat dishes, 10 poultry dishes, 10 seafood dishes, 10 vegetable dishes, 10 side dishes, 10 appetizers, and 10 dessert dishes. I hope you enjoy cooking and eating these dishes as much as I did creating and taste-testing them.

But, before we dive into the recipes, let me tell you why the Mediterranean diet is not just delicious, but also incredibly good for you! You see, people who live in the Mediterranean region have some of the longest life expectancies and the lowest rates of chronic diseases like heart disease, cancer, and diabetes. And, it's all thanks to the amazing ingredients they use in their cooking.

You see, the Mediterranean diet is all about using fresh, whole foods, like fruits, vegetables, whole grains, legumes, nuts, and seeds. It's heavy on olive oil, which is known for its heart-healthy monounsaturated fats, and low in unhealthy saturated and trans fats. It also includes plenty of fish and seafood, which are packed with omega-3 fatty acids that are good for your heart and brain.

And, the best part? The Mediterranean diet allows for the occasional glass of red wine and even a little bit of dark chocolate! So, let's celebrate the flavors and the benefits of the Mediterranean diet with a fork, a knife, and a smile!

Pasta

1. Spaghetti with Fresh Tomato Sauce

Hey there, foodie friends! Today, I'm sharing one of my absolute favorite recipes with you all - Spaghetti with Fresh Tomato Sauce. This dish is a classic in the Mediterranean, and I've had the privilege of enjoying it many times in the small seaside villages along the coast.

So, let's get to it, shall we? First off, I have to tell you that this recipe is a breeze to make. You'll need about 30 minutes of preparation time and 30 minutes of cooking time, and it'll yield 2-4 servings, depending on your appetite. Trust me, you'll want to eat seconds!

Here's what you'll need:

- 400g spaghetti
- 4 medium-sized ripe tomatoes, chopped
- 2 cloves of garlic, minced
- 2 tablespoons of olive oil
- Salt and pepper, to taste
- Fresh basil leaves, to garnish

Alright, now that you've got all your ingredients, let's get cooking! Boil the spaghetti according to the package instructions, and while that's cooking, heat the olive oil in a large pan over medium heat. Add the minced garlic and cook until fragrant, about 1 minute. Then, add the chopped tomatoes and cook until they're soft, about 10 minutes. Season with salt and pepper to taste.

Once the spaghetti is cooked, drain it and add it to the pan with the tomato sauce. Toss everything together until the spaghetti is evenly coated. Serve with some fresh basil leaves on top for that extra pop of flavor.

Oh, and I have to share a little story about this dish. The first time I tried Spaghetti with Fresh Tomato Sauce was in a small fishing village in the Mediterranean. I remember sitting at a rickety wooden table, overlooking the sea, and digging into this plate of absolute deliciousness. The flavors were so fresh and vibrant, and I couldn't get enough. That's when I knew I had to learn how to make it myself!

And there you have it, folks - Spaghetti with Fresh Tomato Sauce, a true classic of the Mediterranean.

Nutritional Values (per serving, based on 4 servings):

Calories: 480	Cholesterol: 0mg	Dietary Fiber: 5g
Total Fat: 15g	Sodium: 150mg	Sugars: 8g
Saturated Fat: 2g	Total Carbohydrates: 76g	Protein: 14g

Enjoy, and let me know how it turns out! Buon appetito!"

2. Linguine with Clam Sauce

Ah, linguine with clam sauce, the perfect pasta dish for seafood lovers! This dish is super simple to make and only takes about 30 minutes from start to finish, which is perfect for those busy weeknights when you don't have all day to cook.

So, let's gather our ingredients:

- 1 pound linguine
- 3 tablespoons olive oil
- 4 cloves of garlic, minced
- 1/2 teaspoon red pepper flakes (optional)
- 2 cans of chopped clams, drained (juice reserved)
- 1/2 cup white wine
- 2 tablespoons chopped fresh parsley
- Salt and pepper to taste
- Parmesan cheese, grated (optional)

First, we'll start by cooking the linguine according to the package instructions until al dente. While that's cooking, let's move on to the sauce. In a large saucepan, heat the olive oil over medium heat and add in the minced garlic and red pepper flakes (if using). Cook for about 2 minutes until fragrant, being careful not to burn the garlic.

Next, add in the drained clams and the reserved juice from the cans. Let it simmer for a couple of minutes, then pour in the white wine. Bring the mixture to a boil and then reduce the heat to low. Let it simmer for about 5 minutes until the liquid has reduced by half.

Once the sauce is ready, drain the linguine and add it to the saucepan. Toss everything together until the pasta is evenly coated with the sauce. If you like, you can add in some grated Parmesan cheese.

To serve, sprinkle some chopped parsley on top and enjoy! This dish is best enjoyed with a glass of crisp white wine and some crusty bread for mopping up all that delicious sauce.

Oh, and here's a little fun fact: in Italy, clams are often referred to as "vongole," which means "little tongues." So, when you're eating linguine with clam sauce, you're basically eating little tongues with little tongues. How fun is that?!

This recipe serves 2-4 people, and each serving contains approximately:

438 calories	53g carbohydrates	3g fiber
17g fat	18g protein	2g sugar.

3. Pasta alla Norma

Ah, Pasta alla Norma, one of my favorite pasta dishes from the beautiful island of Sicily. The combination of the juicy and flavorful eggplant, fresh tomatoes, and a sprinkle of ricotta salata cheese is just heavenly.

And let me tell you a little secret, this dish was named after the famous opera "Norma" by Vincenzo Bellini. The locals would often say, "Bellissima, come la pasta alla Norma" meaning "Beautiful, just like the pasta alla Norma." I mean, who wouldn't want their food to be compared to an opera, right?

Okay, enough with the history lessons, let's get to cooking! Preparation time is about 15 minutes, cooking time is 25 minutes, and it will make 2 to 4 servings, depending on how much you love eggplant.

For this recipe, you will need:

- 1 large eggplant (about 1 lb)
- 1 lb of pasta (linguine or spaghetti)
- 1 can of San Marzano tomatoes (28 oz)
- 4 cloves of garlic
- 1/2 cup of olive oil
- Salt and pepper to taste
- 1/2 cup of fresh basil leaves
- 1/2 cup of ricotta salata cheese, grated

Start by slicing your eggplant into rounds and sprinkle with salt. Let it sit for 15 minutes and then rinse with water and pat dry. This will help reduce the bitterness.

Meanwhile, cook the pasta according to the package instructions and drain. In a pan, heat the olive oil over medium heat and add the sliced garlic. Cook until fragrant, about 2 minutes, and then add the canned tomatoes and a pinch of salt and pepper. Let it simmer for 10 minutes.

In another pan, heat more olive oil and cook the eggplant slices until golden brown on both sides.

Now it's time to assemble the dish! On a large serving platter, spread some tomato sauce, add the cooked pasta, and then the eggplant slices. Pour some more tomato sauce on top, sprinkle with basil leaves and grated ricotta salata cheese.

Serve with some crusty bread and enjoy the flavors of Sicily right in your own kitchen!

Nutritional values (per serving, 2 servings):

Calories: 708	Cholesterol: 13 mg	Dietary Fiber: 11 g
Total Fat: 32 g	Sodium: 889 mg	Sugar: 15 g
Saturated Fat: 5 g	Total Carbohydrates: 95 g	Protein: 19 g

4. Penne alla ~~Vodka~~ Norma

Ah, Pasta alla Norma, one of my favorite pasta dishes from the beautiful island of Sicily. The combination of the juicy and flavorful eggplant, fresh tomatoes, and a sprinkle of ricotta salata cheese is just heavenly.

And let me tell you a little secret, this dish was named after the famous opera "Norma" by Vincenzo Bellini. The locals would often say, "Bellissima, come la pasta alla Norma" meaning "Beautiful, just like the pasta alla Norma." I mean, who wouldn't want their food to be compared to an opera, right?

Okay, enough with the history lessons, let's get to cooking! Preparation time is about 15 minutes, cooking time is 25 minutes, and it will make 2 to 4 servings, depending on how much you love eggplant.

For this recipe, you will need:

- 1 large eggplant (about 1 lb)
- 1 lb of pasta (linguine or spaghetti)
- 1 can of San Marzano tomatoes (28 oz)
- 4 cloves of garlic
- 1/2 cup of olive oil
- Salt and pepper to taste
- 1/2 cup of fresh basil leaves
- 1/2 cup of ricotta salata cheese, grated

Start by slicing your eggplant into rounds and sprinkle with salt. Let it sit for 15 minutes and then rinse with water and pat dry. This will help reduce the bitterness.

Meanwhile, cook the pasta according to the package instructions and drain. In a pan, heat the olive oil over medium heat and add the sliced garlic. Cook until fragrant, about 2 minutes, and then add the canned tomatoes and a pinch of salt and pepper. Let it simmer for 10 minutes.

In another pan, heat more olive oil and cook the eggplant slices until golden brown on both sides.

Now it's time to assemble the dish! On a large serving platter, spread some tomato sauce, add the cooked pasta, and then the eggplant slices. Pour some more tomato sauce on top, sprinkle with basil leaves and grated ricotta salata cheese.

Serve with some crusty bread and enjoy the flavors of Sicily right in your own kitchen!

Nutritional values (per serving, 2 servings):

Calories: 708	Cholesterol: 13 mg	Dietary Fiber: 11 g
Total Fat: 32 g	Sodium: 889 mg	Sugar: 15 g
Saturated Fat: 5 g	Total Carbohydrates: 95 g	Protein: 19 g

5. Fettuccine Alfredo

Hello folks, let me tell you a story about a dish that has been causing confusion since the day it was invented. It's called Fettuccine Alfredo and it's a pasta dish that'll have you saying "Mamma Mia!" with every bite.

Here's what you'll need for 2-4 servings:

- 8 ounces of fettuccine pasta
- 1 cup of heavy cream
- 1/2 cup of grated parmesan cheese
- 2 tablespoons of unsalted butter
- Salt and pepper to taste
- A pinch of nutmeg (optional)

Preparation time: 10 minutes. Cooking time: 15 minutes.

Start by cooking the pasta according to the package instructions, then drain it and set it aside.

In a saucepan, melt the butter over low heat, then add the heavy cream and let it warm up. When the cream starts to bubble, add the grated parmesan cheese and whisk until everything is well combined. Season with salt, pepper, and nutmeg if you like.

Now it's time to bring everything together! Add the cooked pasta to the saucepan and toss everything together until the pasta is well coated. That's it, your Fettuccine Alfredo is ready to be served.

And now for the funny part. It is said that this dish was created by a restaurateur named Alfredo Di Lelio in Rome, Italy, who wanted to make a dish that would satisfy his pregnant wife's cravings for something creamy and comforting. And boy did he hit the jackpot with this one! I mean, who wouldn't love pasta smothered in creamy, cheesy sauce?

Here are the relevant nutritional values for 1 serving (based on 4 servings):

Calories: 483	Cholesterol: 140 mg	Dietary Fiber: 1.5 g
Total Fat: 37.2 g	Sodium: 447 mg	Sugars: 2.3 g
Saturated Fat: 22.4 g	Total Carbohydrates: 27.9 g	Protein: 14.3 g

So, the next time you're in the mood for something creamy and comforting, give Fettuccine Alfredo a try! You won't regret it, I promise. Ciao for now!

6. Spaghetti with Meatballs

Oh boy, Spaghetti with Meatballs is a classic dish that always brings a smile to my face! This dish is perfect for when you're craving comfort food, but want to stay true to the Mediterranean Diet.

Here's what you'll need:

- 1 pound of ground beef or turkey
- 1/2 cup of breadcrumbs
- 1/4 cup of grated Parmesan cheese
- 1 egg
- 1 tablespoon of chopped fresh parsley
- 1 tablespoon of chopped fresh basil
- 1 teaspoon of salt
- 1/2 teaspoon of black pepper
- 1 can of diced tomatoes
- 1/2 cup of heavy cream
- 1 pound of spaghetti
- 2-4 servings

Prep time: 10 minutes

Cooking time: 30 minutes

To start, let's make the meatballs. In a large bowl, mix together the ground beef or turkey, breadcrumbs, Parmesan cheese, egg, parsley, basil, salt, and pepper. Roll the mixture into balls, about 1 1/2 inches in diameter.

Next, heat a large skillet over medium heat. Add the meatballs to the skillet and cook until they're browned on all sides, about 8-10 minutes.

While the meatballs are cooking, let's make the tomato sauce. In a medium saucepan, heat the diced tomatoes over medium heat. Once the tomatoes are hot, add the heavy cream to the pan and stir to combine.

Once the meatballs are fully cooked, add the tomato sauce to the skillet with the meatballs. Let the sauce simmer for 5-10 minutes, until it's heated through.

Now it's time to cook the spaghetti. Fill a large pot with water and bring it to a boil. Add the spaghetti to the pot and cook for 8-10 minutes, or until it's al dente. Drain the spaghetti and add it to a serving dish.

Finally, spoon the meatballs and tomato sauce over the spaghetti. Serve hot and enjoy!

And, I have to tell you an anecdote about Spaghetti with Meatballs. My husband, who's not very adventurous when it comes to food, once told me that he'd only eat Spaghetti with Meatballs if there were, in fact, meatballs involved. So, I made him a plate with just spaghetti and tomato sauce, and he was convinced it was the dish he asked for! He took a bite and said, "Where are the meatballs?" I couldn't stop laughing. Lesson learned, always read the menu carefully!

Nutritional values per serving (based on 4 servings):

Cal: 675

Carbs: 69g

Sodium: 905mg

Fat: 34g

Protein: 38g

7. Pesto Pasta

Ah, Pesto Pasta. The dish that's just as green as the rolling hills of Genoa, the birthplace of pesto. It's the perfect meal for a warm summer day, or for when you want to transport yourself to the Ligurian coast, even if it's just for a few bites.

To make this delicious dish, you'll need the following ingredients for 2-4 servings:

1. 1 lb. of pasta of your choice (I prefer linguine or spaghetti)
2. 1 cup of fresh basil leaves
3. 1/2 cup of freshly grated Parmesan cheese
4. 1/2 cup of extra-virgin olive oil
5. 1/3 cup of pine nuts (or you can use almonds if you can't find pine nuts)
6. 4 garlic cloves, peeled
7. Salt and pepper, to taste

First, bring a large pot of salted water to a boil. Once it's boiling, add your pasta and cook until al dente, following the instructions on the package. Reserve 1 cup of the pasta cooking water.

While the pasta is cooking, it's time to make the pesto! In a food processor or blender, combine the basil, Parmesan, olive oil, pine nuts, garlic, salt, and pepper. Blend until you have a smooth and creamy sauce. If it's too thick, add a little bit of the pasta cooking water until you reach the desired consistency.

Once the pasta is ready, drain it and return it to the pot. Add the pesto sauce and toss well to evenly coat the pasta. Serve immediately, garnished with some extra grated Parmesan and a drizzle of olive oil, if desired.

And now, let me share a little anecdote with you. The first time I made Pesto Pasta, I was so proud of myself. I thought I had created a masterpiece. But, when I served it to my husband, he took one bite and said, "It's good, but it's not as good as Nonna's." Nonna, of course, being his grandmother who's an amazing cook. I was crushed. But, you know what, I didn't let that get me down. I kept practicing and now, I'm happy to say, my Pesto Pasta is just as good as Nonna's, or even better if I do say so myself!

Nutritional values (per serving based on 4 servings):

Calories: 711   Saturated Fat: 11 g   Fiber: 2 g

Fat: 63 g   Carbohydrates: 31 g   Protein: 13 g

8. Orecchiette with Broccoli Rabe and Sausage

Orecchiette with Broccoli Rabe and Sausage, it's a perfect match made in heaven, I mean, pasta heaven! This dish is perfect for a quick and easy weeknight dinner, but it's also special enough for a dinner party. Trust me, your guests will be impressed.

So, let's get started. You will need the following ingredients:

- 1 pound of orecchiette pasta
- 1 head of broccoli rabe, trimmed and chopped
- 4 Italian sausages, casings removed
- 4 cloves of garlic, minced
- 1/4 cup of olive oil
- Salt and pepper to taste
- 1 cup of grated parmesan cheese
- Red pepper flakes (optional)

Preparation time: 15 minutes. Cooking time: 25 minutes. Serves 4.

Now let's cook! Start by bringing a large pot of salted water to a boil. Cook the pasta according to the package instructions until it's al dente. Reserve 1 cup of pasta water and drain the rest.

In a large skillet, heat the olive oil over medium heat. Add the sausage and cook until browned and crispy, about 8 minutes. Add the minced garlic and cook for another minute until fragrant.

Next, add the chopped broccoli rabe to the skillet and cook until tender, about 5 minutes. Season with salt and pepper to taste.

Now, it's time to bring everything together. Add the cooked pasta and reserved pasta water to the skillet. Toss everything together until the pasta is coated in the sauce.

Sprinkle the grated parmesan cheese over the pasta and continue to toss until the cheese is melted and the pasta is coated.

And voilà! Your Orecchiette with Broccoli Rabe and Sausage is ready to be served. You can add a sprinkle of red pepper flakes for a little extra heat.

I have a funny story about this dish. Once, I was cooking this for my family and I got so excited that I overcooked the broccoli rabe. My husband took one bite and said, "This tastes like grass." I was so embarrassed, but my kids loved it and asked for seconds. So, now I always make sure to not overcook the broccoli rabe!

Nutritional values (per serving, based on 4 servings):

Calories: 757	Cholesterol: 68mg	Fiber: 5g
Fat: 38g	Sodium: 586mg	Sugar: 4g
Saturated Fat: 12g	Carbohydrates: 69g	Protein: 27g

9. Stuffed Shells

Sure thing! Here's my take on Stuffed Shells, in a narrative and fun style:

"Oh boy, get ready for a feast, because today we're making some delicious Stuffed Shells! This classic Italian dish is a crowd-pleaser and a staple in every Italian grandma's kitchen, including mine. I learned how to make it from my nonna, who used to make it for special occasions.

We start with jumbo pasta shells, the bigger the better, and stuff them with a creamy mixture of ricotta cheese, parmesan cheese, and fresh herbs. The combination of the soft, fluffy ricotta and the nutty, salty parmesan creates a heavenly filling that will make you want to eat the whole pan. And the herbs, they add a freshness and lightness that makes this dish irresistible.

Here's what you'll need to make this recipe:

- 12 ounces jumbo pasta shells
- 1 cup ricotta cheese
- 1/2 cup grated parmesan cheese
- 2 tablespoons chopped fresh basil
- 2 tablespoons chopped fresh parsley
- Salt and pepper, to taste
- Your favorite marinara sauce
- Shredded mozzarella cheese, to top (optional)

To make this dish, preheat your oven to 375°F. Cook the pasta shells according to the package instructions until they're al dente, then drain and set aside. In a bowl, mix together the ricotta cheese, parmesan cheese, basil, parsley, salt, and pepper. Fill each pasta shell with about a tablespoon of the cheese mixture and place them in a baking dish. Pour the marinara sauce over the stuffed shells and sprinkle shredded mozzarella cheese on top, if desired. Bake for 25-30 minutes or until the cheese is melted and bubbly.

And there you have it, folks! A classic Italian dish that will transport you straight to Italy. You can serve these Stuffed Shells as a main course or as a side dish, and they pair well with a simple salad and a glass of red wine. Enjoy, and Buon Appetito!

As for anecdotes, I always like to add a little twist to my stuffed shells. One time, I had some leftover chicken and decided to chop it up and mix it into the ricotta mixture. My family went wild for the added protein and flavor. I like to call them my "power stuffed shells."

Nutritional values (per serving, based on 4 servings):

Calories: 352	Cholesterol: 46mg	Fiber: 2.3g
Fat: 15.4g	Sodium: 664mg	Sugar: 5.7g
Saturated Fat: 8.2g	Carbohydrates: 36.2g	Protein: 17.4g

10. Pasta with Sun-Dried Tomato and Olive Pesto

Ahh, Pasta with Sun-Dried Tomato and Olive Pesto! Now this is a dish that just screams "Mediterranean" with its bold and robust flavors. You know what they say, if life gives you sun-dried tomatoes and olives, make pesto!

So here's what you'll need for this recipe:
-1 pound of your favorite pasta
-1 cup of sun-dried tomatoes packed in oil, drained
-1/2 cup of pitted Kalamata olives
-1/2 cup of freshly grated Parmesan cheese
-1/2 cup of extra-virgin olive oil
-2 cloves of garlic, minced
-1/2 teaspoon of red pepper flakes (optional)
-Salt and pepper to taste

Start by boiling your pasta al dente in a large pot of salted water. While your pasta is cooking, let's make the pesto!
In a food processor, combine the sun-dried tomatoes, olives, Parmesan cheese, olive oil, garlic, and red pepper flakes (if using). Pulse until smooth and combined. Season with salt and pepper to taste.

Once your pasta is ready, drain and return it back to the pot. Add the pesto to the pasta and stir until the pasta is coated in the sauce.

Serve the pasta hot and garnish with additional grated Parmesan cheese and some freshly chopped parsley, if desired.

Now, here's an anecdote for you: I once served this dish to my Italian grandmother who was visiting from Napoli and she said it was the best pasta she's had since she left Italy! Can you believe it? This dish is not just delicious, but it's also got a seal of approval from a real Italian nonna!

Nutritional Values (per serving, assuming 4 servings):

Calories: 468   Protein: 14g   Fiber: 4g

Fat: 28g   Carbohydrates: 45g   Sugar: 4g

Soups

11. Lentil Soup with Kale and Carrots

Hi everyone! It's Maria, and today we're making one of my favorite healthy and hearty dishes: Lentil Soup with Kale and Carrots. This is the perfect meal for a cold winter day, and it's packed with flavor and nutrition.

So, let's get started! First, let's gather our ingredients. We'll need:

- 1 cup brown or green lentils, rinsed and drained
- 6 cups vegetable or chicken broth
- 2 medium carrots, peeled and diced
- 1 large onion, diced
- 2 cloves garlic, minced
- 2 cups kale, chopped
- 1 teaspoon dried thyme
- 1 teaspoon dried rosemary
- Salt and pepper, to taste
- 2 tablespoons olive oil

Now, let's get cooking! In a large pot, heat the olive oil over medium heat. Add the onion, garlic, and carrots and sauté until the onion is translucent, about 5 minutes. Then, add the lentils, vegetable broth, thyme, rosemary, and salt and pepper to the pot. Stir everything together and bring the soup to a boil. Reduce the heat and let the soup simmer for 25-30 minutes, or until the lentils are tender.

Finally, add the kale to the soup and let it cook for another 5 minutes. And that's it! Your Lentil Soup with Kale and Carrots is now ready to serve.

Now, let's talk about the nutrition. This delicious soup contains about 250 calories per serving and is packed with protein, fiber, vitamins, and minerals. It's the perfect meal to help you stay full and energized all day long.

And now, an anecdote. One time, I made this soup for a friend who was feeling under the weather, and they said it was like a warm hug in a bowl. So, if you're looking for a comforting and nutritious meal, give this Lentil Soup with Kale and Carrots a try! I promise, you won't regret it.

Nutritional Values (per serving, assuming 2 servings):

Calories: 300	Sodium: 640mg	Protein: 17g
Fat: 7g	Carbohydrates: 44g	Fiber: 20g

12. Minestrone Soup with Tomatoes, Zucchini, and Beans

Sure thing! Let me redo the recipe for "Minestrone Soup with Tomatoes, Zucchini, and Beans" in the desired format:

"Ah, Minestrone Soup with Tomatoes, Zucchini, and Beans, the ultimate comfort food. This dish is a staple in every Italian household and has been passed down from generations to generations. It's the perfect soup for a chilly day, or when you want to warm up your heart and soul.

Now, let's talk ingredients. You'll need:

- 2 tablespoons olive oil
- 1 large onion, diced
- 2 cloves garlic, minced
- 2 large carrots, peeled and diced
- 2 stalks celery, diced
- 2 medium zucchini, diced
- 1 can diced tomatoes (28 ounces)
- 4 cups vegetable broth
- 1 can kidney beans (15 ounces), drained and rinsed
- 1 cup small pasta, such as ditalini
- 1 teaspoon dried basil
- 1 teaspoon dried oregano
- Salt and pepper, to taste
- 2 cups chopped kale
- 1/4 cup grated parmesan cheese, plus more for serving

And now, let's talk preparation time and cooking time. This beauty of a soup will only take you 15 minutes to prepare and 30 minutes to cook, so it's the perfect quick and easy dinner option. Plus, it makes great leftovers, so you can enjoy it for lunch the next day too.

So, let's get started! In a large saucepan, heat the olive oil over medium heat. Add the onion, garlic, carrots, and celery, and cook until the vegetables are soft and the onion is translucent, about 8 minutes. Add the zucchini, diced tomatoes, vegetable broth, kidney beans, pasta, basil, oregano, salt, and pepper. Bring to a boil, then reduce the heat to low, cover, and simmer until the pasta is cooked, about 15 minutes. Stir in the kale and parmesan cheese, and cook until the kale is wilted, about 3 minutes.

And now, the moment of truth, the nutritional values! For each serving, you'll get:

Calories: 250	Sodium: 830mg	Fiber: 6g
Fat: 10g	Carbohydrates: 33g	Protein: 12g

So there you have it, folks! A delicious, nutritious, and hearty Minestrone Soup with Tomatoes, Zucchini, and Beans that will warm your heart and soul. Serve with a sprinkle of parmesan cheese and a piece of crusty bread, and enjoy!"

13. Tomato and Basil Soup with Croutons

Ah, Tomato and Basil Soup with Croutons! A classic Italian dish that's both simple and satisfying. Let me tell you, this soup is the epitome of comfort food and will warm you up on a cold winter's night.

So, gather up the ingredients! You'll need:

- 2 tablespoons olive oil1 onion, diced
- 2 garlic cloves, minced
- 2 cans (28 ounces each) whole peeled tomatoes
- 4 cups chicken or vegetable broth
- 1/4 cup fresh basil leaves, plus more for serving
- Salt and freshly ground black pepper
- 1/2 cup breadcrumbs
- 1/4 cup freshly grated Parmesan cheese
- 2 tablespoons unsalted butter

Now let's get started! Heat the olive oil in a large pot over medium heat. Add the onion and garlic and cook until soft, about 5 minutes. Add the tomatoes and their juice, broth, and basil leaves. Season with salt and pepper, to taste.

Bring the soup to a simmer and let it cook for about 15 minutes. Use an immersion blender to puree the soup until smooth. If you don't have an immersion blender, you can carefully transfer the soup to a blender and puree in batches.

Now for the croutons! Preheat the oven to 375°F (190°C). In a small bowl, mix together the breadcrumbs, Parmesan cheese, and melted butter. Spread the mixture evenly on a baking sheet and bake until golden brown, about 10 minutes.

Ladle the soup into bowls, top with the croutons, and a few fresh basil leaves. Serve hot and enjoy!

Now, here's a little secret. My Nonna (grandma) always added a drizzle of olive oil on top of each bowl. It makes the soup extra rich and delicious. You should try it, you won't regret it!

Nutritional values per serving:

Calories: 243	Cholesterol: 20mg	Fiber: 4g
Total Fat: 17g	Sodium: 577mg	Sugar: 6g
Saturated Fat: 5g	Carbohydrates: 18g	Protein: 7g

14. Chickpea and Spinach Soup with Lemon

Ah, it's time for another delicious and healthy soup recipe! This one is a real crowd-pleaser and perfect for those days when you want something warm and comforting. Introducing, the Chickpea and Spinach Soup with Lemon!

So, let's get started. First things first, let's gather the ingredients:

- 1 onion, chopped
- 3 garlic cloves, minced
- 1 tablespoon olive oil
- 2 cans of chickpeas, drained and rinsed
- 4 cups vegetable broth
- 3 cups fresh spinach
- 1 teaspoon dried basil
- Salt and pepper to taste
- 2 tablespoons lemon juice

Now, let me share a little anecdote with you. Whenever I make this soup, my husband always says, "It smells so good, I could eat a bowl right now!" And let me tell you, the smell alone is enough to make your mouth water.

Okay, let's get cooking! In a large pot, heat the olive oil over medium heat. Add the onion and garlic, and cook for about 3-4 minutes or until the onion is translucent. Add the chickpeas, vegetable broth, basil, salt, and pepper. Bring the soup to a boil and then reduce the heat and let it simmer for about 15 minutes. Add the spinach and lemon juice and let it cook for another 2-3 minutes or until the spinach is wilted.

And that's it! This soup is so easy to make and it's packed with flavor and nutrients. You can serve it with some crusty bread or croutons to make it even more delicious.

Now, let's talk about the nutritional values. For 2 servings, each serving has:

Calories: 239	Sodium: 789 mg	Fiber: 9 g
Fat: 6 g	Carbohydrates: 37 g	Protein: 12 g

So, there you have it! A delicious, healthy, and satisfying soup that's perfect for those chilly days. Give it a try and let me know what you think!

15. Roasted Red Pepper Soup with Feta and Herbs

Ah, "Roasted Red Pepper Soup with Feta and Herbs." It's a soup so good, you'll want to eat it even when it's not chilly outside! But don't do that, okay? That's just weird.

So, I remember when I first made this Roasted Red Pepper Soup with Feta and Herbs, my family couldn't get enough of it. They kept asking for seconds, thirds, and even fourths! It was a big hit and since then, it's become one of our favorite soups. But the real star of the show here are the roasted red peppers, they add the perfect sweetness and depth of flavor to this soup. And with a sprinkle of feta and herbs, it just elevates the whole dish to another level. Trust me, this soup is a real crowd-pleaser, and you won't be disappointed!

For this delicious and comforting dish, you'll need:

- 4 red bell peppers
- 1 large onion
- 3 cloves of garlic
- 1 tablespoon olive oil
- 1 cup vegetable broth
- 1/2 teaspoon paprika
- Salt and pepper, to taste
- 1/4 teaspoon dried thyme
- 1/4 teaspoon dried basil
- 1/4 cup crumbled feta cheese
- 2 tablespoons chopped fresh parsley

First, let's start with the red bell peppers. You're gonna love this part, because you get to play with fire! Roast the peppers over an open flame, using tongs to rotate them, until their skins are blackened and blistered. Or, if you're like me and don't like playing with fire, you can also roast them in a 400°F oven for about 30 minutes.

Once the peppers are roasted, let them cool for a bit, then peel the skin off and remove the seeds and stems. Cut the peppers into small pieces.

Next, heat the olive oil in a large pot over medium heat. Add the onion and garlic and cook until they are soft and fragrant, about 5 minutes.

Add the vegetable broth, paprika, thyme, basil, and roasted red peppers to the pot. Season with salt and pepper to taste. Bring the mixture to a boil, then reduce the heat and let it simmer for about 10 minutes.

Use an immersion blender to puree the soup until it's smooth. If you don't have an immersion blender, you can also transfer the soup to a blender and puree it in batches.

Serve the soup hot, topped with crumbled feta cheese and chopped fresh parsley. Enjoy your warm and comforting bowl of "Roasted Red Pepper Soup with Feta and Herbs."

Nutritional Values per serving (4 servings):

Calories: 124

Total Fat: 9g

Saturated Fat: 4g

Cholesterol: 18mg

Sodium: 483mg

Total Carbohydrates: 10g

Dietary Fiber: 3g

Sugars: 4g

Protein: 4g

16. Carrot and Ginger Soup with a Hint of Harissa

Certainly, I apologize for any confusion. Let me redo the recipe for you in the format we agreed on.

Ah, Carrot and Ginger Soup with a Hint of Harissa! Now this is a warm, comforting bowl of goodness that is sure to brighten up your day. The combination of juicy, sweet carrots and zesty ginger, with just a touch of the spicy and smoky Harissa, will have your taste buds doing the tango!

So, what do we need? Well, let's see:

- 6 medium carrots, peeled and chopped
- 2 inches of fresh ginger, peeled and minced
- 1 large onion, diced
- 2 cloves of garlic, minced
- 4 cups of vegetable broth
- 1 tablespoon of Harissa paste
- Salt and pepper, to taste
- 2 tablespoons of olive oil

Fresh herbs such as cilantro, parsley, or chives, for garnish (optional)

Lemon wedges, for serving (optional)

To start, heat the olive oil in a large pot over medium heat. Add the onion, garlic, and ginger, and sauté for a few minutes, until the onion is translucent. Next, add the chopped carrots and continue to cook for another 5 minutes, stirring occasionally.

Pour in the vegetable broth, bring everything to a boil, then reduce heat and let it simmer for 20 minutes, or until the carrots are tender.

Now it's time to add the Harissa paste! Give it a good stir, and let it simmer for another 5 minutes.

Once everything is cooked, use an immersion blender to puree the soup until smooth. You can also transfer the soup in batches to a blender or food processor to puree. Season with salt and pepper to taste.

Your Carrot and Ginger Soup with a Hint of Harissa is now ready to be served! Serve with a squeeze of lemon juice and a sprinkle of fresh herbs, if desired.

Preparation Time: 15 minutes

Cooking Time: 30 minutes

Servings: 4

Nutritional Information (per serving):

Calories: 170	Carbs: 19g	Fiber: 5g
Fat: 11g	Protein: 4g	

There you have it! A delicious and healthy bowl of soup that will warm your belly and your heart. Enjoy!

17. Chicken and Rice Soup with Lemon and Oregano

I apologize for not including an anecdote in the previous recipe. Here's a revised version of the recipe with an anecdote included:

"Chicken and Rice Soup with Lemon and Oregano, a warm and comforting soup that's perfect for when you're feeling under the weather or just need a bowl of coziness. This dish is a classic and has been around for generations, passed down from mothers to daughters, and has become a staple in many households.

Do you know why I love this soup? Because it takes me back to my childhood when my grandmother used to make it for me whenever I was feeling down. She would always add a pinch of love and a squeeze of lemon, and it would always make me feel better.

Now, let's talk ingredients. You'll need:

- 2 tablespoons olive oil
- 1 onion, diced
- 2 cloves garlic, minced
- 2 carrots, peeled and diced
- 2 stalks celery, diced
- 4 cups chicken broth
- 1 cup long grain rice
- 1 pound boneless chicken breast, cut into small pieces
- 1 lemon, zested and juiced
- 1 teaspoon dried oregano
- Salt and pepper, to taste

And now, let's talk preparation time and cooking time. This lovely soup will only take you 15 minutes to prepare and 20 minutes to cook, making it the perfect quick and easy dinner option. Plus, it makes great leftovers, so you can enjoy it for lunch the next day too.

So, let's get started! In a large saucepan, heat the olive oil over medium heat. Add the onion, garlic, carrots, and celery, and cook until the vegetables are soft and the onion is translucent, about 8 minutes. Add the chicken broth, rice, chicken, lemon zest, lemon juice, oregano, salt, and pepper. Bring to a boil, then reduce the heat to low, cover, and simmer until the rice is cooked and the chicken is no longer pink, about 20 minutes.

And now, the moment of truth, the nutritional values! For each serving, you'll get:

Calories: 380   Sodium: 830mg   Fiber: 2g

Fat: 8g   Carbohydrates: 45g   Protein: 29g

So there you have it, folks! A delicious, nutritious, and comforting Chicken and Rice Soup with Lemon and Oregano that will warm your heart and soul. Serve with a squeeze of lemon and a slice of crusty bread, and enjoy!

18. Fish Soup with Clams, Mussels, and Shrimp

Fish Soup with Clams, Mussels, and Shrimp, now this is a dish that takes me back to my childhood summers spent by the coast. My grandmother would make this soup for us every time we visited her, and the aroma of fresh seafood and herbs cooking together would fill the whole house.

Let's talk ingredients, shall we? You'll need:

- 2 tablespoons olive oil
- 1 large onion, diced
- 2 cloves garlic, minced
- 2 medium carrots, peeled and diced
- 2 stalks celery, diced
- 1 cup white wine
- 4 cups fish stock
- 1 can diced tomatoes (28 ounces)
- 1 lb mixed seafood (clams, mussels, and shrimp)
- 2 teaspoons dried thyme
- 2 teaspoons dried basil
- Salt and pepper, to taste
- 1/4 cup chopped fresh parsley

And now, let's talk about the preparation and cooking time. This soup is incredibly quick and easy to make, taking only 15 minutes to prepare and 30 minutes to cook. The best part? You get to enjoy a bowl of this delicious soup in no time!

Let's get started! In a large saucepan, heat the olive oil over medium heat. Add the onion, garlic, carrots, and celery, and cook until the vegetables are soft and the onion is translucent, about 8 minutes. Add the white wine and let it simmer for 2 minutes, then add the fish stock, diced tomatoes, mixed seafood, thyme, basil, salt, and pepper. Bring to a boil, then reduce the heat to low, cover, and simmer until the seafood is cooked, about 15 minutes. Stir in the parsley and serve hot.

And now, let's talk about the nutritional values. For each serving, you'll get:

Calories: 250	Sodium: 830mg	Fiber: 2g
Fat: 10g	Carbohydrates: 15g	Protein: 28g

So there you have it, folks! A delicious, nutritious, and comforting Fish Soup with Clams, Mussels, and Shrimp, straight from the coast. Serve with a piece of crusty bread, and enjoy the memories!

19. Broccoli and Stilton Soup with a Drizzle of Olive Oil

Ah, Broccoli and Stilton Soup with a Drizzle of Olive Oil, the perfect soup for a cozy night in. This soup is a delightful blend of rich, creamy stilton cheese and tender, nutty broccoli, all brought together with a touch of olive oil to add a gentle, fruity flavor.

Now, let's talk ingredients. You'll need:

- 2 tablespoons olive oil
- 1 large onion, diced
- 2 cloves garlic, minced
- 1 head broccoli, cut into florets
- 4 cups chicken or vegetable broth
- 1/2 cup heavy cream
- 4 ounces stilton cheese, crumbled
- Salt and pepper, to taste

For a crispy topping, you'll also need:

- 1/4 cup breadcrumbs
- 2 tablespoons olive oil

And now, let's talk preparation time and cooking time. This delicious soup will only take you 15 minutes to prepare and 25 minutes to cook, so it's the perfect dinner option for a busy weeknight. And, as an added bonus, it makes great leftovers, so you can enjoy it for lunch the next day too.

Now, onto the fun part - cooking! In a large saucepan, heat the olive oil over medium heat. Add the onion and garlic, and cook until the onion is translucent, about 5 minutes. Add the broccoli and broth, and bring to a boil. Reduce the heat to low, cover, and simmer until the broccoli is tender, about 15 minutes.

While the soup is cooking, make the crispy topping. In a small bowl, mix together the breadcrumbs and olive oil. Set aside.

Once the soup is done cooking, puree it with an immersion blender or transfer it to a blender or food processor and puree until smooth. Stir in the cream and stilton cheese, and season with salt and pepper to taste.

Here's a fun little anecdote to make you smile while you're enjoying this delicious soup. Did you know that stilton cheese has been known to cause "stilton dreams"? That's right, many people report having vivid, colorful dreams after eating this blue-veined cheese. So, enjoy your soup and maybe you'll dream about a land filled with endless broccoli and stilton soup!

And now, the moment of truth, the nutritional values! For each serving, you'll get:

Calories: 420   Sodium: 720mg   Fiber: 3g

Fat: 36g   Carbohydrates: 12g   Protein: 14

So there you have it, folks! A delicious, creamy Broccoli and Stilton Soup with a Drizzle of Olive Oil that's sure to warm your heart and soul. Serve with a sprinkle of the crispy breadcrumb topping and enjoy!

20. Gazpacho with Cucumber, Red Bell Pepper, and Breadcrumbs

Gazpacho, the refreshing summer soup that will transport you to the sunny streets of Spain. This dish is the perfect way to cool down on a hot day and enjoy the flavors of the season.

Now, let's talk ingredients. You'll need:

- 6 ripe large tomatoes, peeled and chopped
- 1 large cucumber, peeled and chopped
- 1 red bell pepper, chopped
- 1/2 red onion, chopped
- 2 cloves garlic, minced
- 2 tablespoons red wine vinegar
- 1/4 cup olive oil, plus more for drizzling
- 2 slices white bread, crusts removed and bread torn into pieces
- 2 cups vegetable broth

Salt and pepper, to taste

And now, let's talk preparation time and cooking time. This delicious and healthy gazpacho will take you just 10 minutes to prepare and 2 hours to chill, making it the perfect make-ahead option for your next summer get-together.

Now, here's a little anecdote about Gazpacho. It's said that back in the day, farm workers in Spain would enjoy a bowl of Gazpacho to beat the heat during their lunch break. The soup was made with whatever ingredients were on hand, including stale bread, which helped to thicken the soup. And that, my friends, is how this timeless classic was born.

So, let's get started! In a blender or food processor, combine the tomatoes, cucumber, red bell pepper, red onion, garlic, red wine vinegar, olive oil, bread, vegetable broth, salt, and pepper. Blend until smooth. Chill in the refrigerator for at least 2 hours, or overnight.

And now, the moment of truth, the nutritional values! For each serving, you'll get:

Calories: 140   Sodium: 320mg   Fiber: 2g

Fat: 11g   Carbohydrates: 11g   Protein: 3g

So there you have it, folks! A delicious, nutritious, and refreshing Gazpacho that will transport you to the sunny streets of Spain. Drizzle with a bit of olive oil, and enjoy

Salads

21. Grilled Eggplant and Tomato Salad

Ah, Grilled Eggplant and Tomato Salad, the perfect combination of smoky, juicy, and fresh flavors! This dish is a staple in Mediterranean cuisine and is often served as a side or as a light main course. It's the perfect dish for a warm summer day, or when you want to enjoy the taste of the season.

Now, let's talk ingredients. You'll need:

- 1 large eggplant, sliced
- 1 large tomato, sliced
- 2 tablespoons olive oil
- 1 tablespoon balsamic vinegar
- 2 cloves garlic, minced
- 1 teaspoon dried basil
- 1 teaspoon dried oregano
- Salt and pepper, to taste
- 1/4 cup breadcrumbs
- 1/4 cup grated parmesan cheese

And now, let's talk preparation time and cooking time. This simple yet delicious salad will only take you 10 minutes to prepare and 10 minutes to grill, so it's the perfect quick and easy dinner option.

So, let's get started! Preheat the grill to medium-high heat. In a large bowl, whisk together the olive oil, balsamic vinegar, garlic, basil, oregano, salt, and pepper. Add the eggplant and tomato slices, and toss to coat.

Grill the eggplant and tomato slices until they are tender and charred, about 5 minutes per side. In a separate small bowl, mix the breadcrumbs and parmesan cheese.

To serve, arrange the grilled eggplant and tomato slices on a serving platter. Sprinkle with the breadcrumb and parmesan cheese mixture.

And now, the moment of truth, the nutritional values! For each serving, you'll get:

Calories: 250	Sodium: 310mg	Fiber: 5g
Fat: 15g	Carbohydrates: 18g	Protein: 8g

So there you have it, folks! A delicious, nutritious, and fresh Grilled Eggplant and Tomato Salad that will satisfy your taste buds and your healthy lifestyle. Serve it with a slice of crusty bread and a glass of chilled white wine, and enjoy!

An anecdote to share with this dish: Did you know that eggplants were once believed to have evil powers and were used as protection against evil spirits? People would carry eggplants with them as talismans, or hang them outside their homes to ward off evil. But now, we just enjoy them as a delicious and nutritious part of our diets!

22. Greek Salad with Cucumber, Tomato, and Feta

Ah, Greek Salad with Cucumber, Tomato, and Feta, the epitome of summer in a bowl. This dish is the perfect addition to any summer barbeque, or when you want to transport yourself to the sunny beaches of Greece. The combination of juicy tomatoes, crisp cucumbers, tangy feta cheese, and a bright dressing is a symphony of flavors that's sure to tantalize your taste buds.

Let's talk ingredients. You'll need:

- 4 ripe tomatoes, chopped
- 1 large cucumber, peeled, seeded and chopped
- 1 red onion, sliced
- 1/2 cup Kalamata olives, pitted
- 1/2 cup crumbled feta cheese
- 1/4 cup olive oil
- 2 tablespoons freshly squeezed lemon juice
- 1 teaspoon dried oregano
- Salt and pepper, to taste

And now, let's talk preparation time and cooking time. This quick and easy salad will only take you 10 minutes to prepare and none to cook, making it the perfect option for busy weeknights or when you're short on time. Plus, it makes a great side dish that can be served cold, so it's perfect for picnics or outdoor events.

So, let's get started! In a large bowl, combine the chopped tomatoes, cucumber, red onion, olives, and feta cheese. In a separate small bowl, whisk together the olive oil, lemon juice, oregano, salt, and pepper. Pour the dressing over the vegetable mixture and toss to coat.

And now, the moment of truth, the nutritional values! For each serving, you'll get:

Calories: 200   Sodium: 360mg   Fiber: 3g

Fat: 16g   Carbohydrates: 12g   Protein: 6g

So there you have it, folks! A delicious, nutritious, and fresh Greek Salad with Cucumber, Tomato, and Feta that will transport your taste buds to the sunny beaches of Greece. Serve with a side of pita bread, and enjoy!

As an anecdote, I once heard of a man who ate Greek Salad for breakfast, lunch, and dinner for an entire week because he just couldn't get enough of its bright and bold flavors. It may sound crazy, but that just shows how irresistible this dish truly is!

23. Tabbouleh with Parsley, Mint, and Bulgur Wheat

Tabbouleh, a traditional Middle Eastern salad that's known for its fresh and vibrant flavors. It's a staple dish in many households and a must-have at any family gathering or special occasion. This delicious salad is not only bursting with flavors but also packed with healthy ingredients.

So, what do you need to bring this dish to life? Here's your grocery list:

- 1 cup bulgur wheat
- 1 cup boiling water
- 1/2 cup fresh parsley, chopped
- 1/4 cup fresh mint, chopped
- 1 large tomato, chopped
- 1 large cucumber, chopped
- 2 tablespoons lemon juice
- 2 tablespoons extra-virgin olive oil
- Salt and pepper, to taste

Making Tabbouleh is as easy as 1, 2, 3. Start by soaking the bulgur wheat in boiling water for about 30 minutes or until it's soft. Then, in a large bowl, mix together the parsley, mint, tomato, cucumber, lemon juice, olive oil, salt, and pepper. Finally, add the bulgur wheat and mix until everything is well combined. And that's it! Your Tabbouleh is ready to be served.

I remember when my grandma used to make this dish for me and my cousins during summer holidays. She would always say that the secret to the best Tabbouleh is to chop all the ingredients as fine as possible. I still follow her advice to this day and it always turns out perfectly.

Each serving of Tabbouleh provides:

Calories: 170   Sodium: 95mg   Fiber: 6g

Fat: 9g   Carbohydrates: 20g   Protein: 5g

Serve Tabbouleh with a fresh piece of pita bread and enjoy its amazing flavor! You won't be disappointed.

24. Caprese Salad with Fresh Mozzarella and Basil

Alright, let's get started with the delicious and refreshing Caprese Salad with Fresh Mozzarella and Basil! To create this classic Italian dish, you'll need the following ingredients:

- 1 pound fresh mozzarella cheese, cut into 1/4-inch slices
- 2 medium ripe tomatoes, cut into 1/4-inch slices
- 1/2 cup fresh basil leaves
- 1/4 cup extra-virgin olive oil
- 2 tablespoons balsamic vinegar
- Salt and pepper, to taste

With regards to timing, this dish takes a total of 15 minutes to prepare and serve. It's perfect for a quick and easy lunch or dinner, or even as a side dish for a special occasion.

The preparation process is simple and straightforward. Start by arranging the mozzarella and tomato slices on a platter, alternating between the two. Then, scatter the basil leaves on top.

Next, in a small bowl, whisk together the olive oil, balsamic vinegar, salt, and pepper. Drizzle the mixture evenly over the salad.

And that's it! Your Caprese Salad with Fresh Mozzarella and Basil is ready to be served and enjoyed.

A little known fact about Caprese Salad is that it was created in the early 20th century on the beautiful island of Capri, off the coast of Italy. The bright and vibrant colors of the ingredients were said to represent the colors of the Italian flag, and it quickly became a popular dish both on the island and throughout Italy.

For those who are watching their calorie intake, here's the nutritional information for a single serving of this dish:

Total Calories: 279   Total Carbohydrates: 10.2 g

Total Fat: 24.5 g   Total Protein: 11.5 g

25. Mediterranean Chickpea Salad with Red Onion and Feta

Introducing a scrumptious delight from the Mediterranean, this Chickpea Salad with Red Onion and Feta is bursting with flavor! A medley of wholesome ingredients, including juicy chickpeas, crisp red onion, and tangy feta cheese, come together to create a healthy and satisfying dish.

Here's what you'll need to whip up this tasty treat:

- 1 can of chickpeas, drained and rinsed
- 1/2 red onion, finely chopped
- 1/2 cup of crumbled feta cheese
- 2 tablespoons of freshly squeezed lemon juice
- 2 tablespoons of extra virgin olive oil
- Salt and pepper, to taste

Preparing this flavorful dish is a breeze. It will take a total of 10 minutes to put together, and the result is 4 servings of yumminess.

First, in a large bowl, combine the chickpeas, red onion, and feta cheese. In a separate small bowl, whisk together the lemon juice, olive oil, salt, and pepper. Pour the dressing over the chickpea mixture, and gently toss to evenly distribute. That's it! Serve immediately or store in the refrigerator until ready to enjoy.

An interesting fact about chickpeas is that they have been a staple food in the Mediterranean for thousands of years. In fact, they are one of the oldest cultivated crops, with evidence of their use dating back to the ancient Egyptians.

Here's a breakdown of the nutritional values per serving:

Calories: 236	Fat: 14g	Saturated Fat: 4g
Saturated Fat: 4g	Fiber: 5g	Cholesterol: 19mg
Sodium: 324mg	Sugar: 2g	
Carbohydrates: 18g	Protein: 9g	

26. Mediterranean Roasted Vegetable Salad with Balsamic Dressing

Introducing the dish, we have a vibrant and flavorful salad that is sure to tantalize your taste buds. With a mix of colorful and healthy veggies roasted to perfection, this salad is a wholesome treat. And to top it off, we have a tangy balsamic dressing that brings all the flavors together.

First up, the ingredients! To make this delicious salad, you'll need:

- 1 eggplant
- 1 red bell pepper
- 1 yellow bell pepper
- 1 red onion
- 1 zucchini
- 1 yellow squash
- 4 cloves of garlic
- Salt and pepper to taste
- 3 tbsp olive oil
- 3 tbsp balsamic vinegar
- 1 tsp honey
- Fresh basil for garnish

Next, let's talk about the cooking time, preparation time and servings. This salad takes about 45 minutes to cook and prepare. You'll be able to serve 4 people with this recipe.

To make this salad, start by preheating your oven to 400°F. Cut the eggplant, red and yellow bell peppers, red onion, zucchini and yellow squash into bite-sized pieces. Mince the garlic. Place the veggies on a baking sheet, drizzle with 2 tablespoons of olive oil and season with salt and pepper. Roast in the oven for 35-40 minutes, until the veggies are tender and slightly charred. In a small bowl, whisk together the remaining 1 tablespoon of olive oil, balsamic vinegar and honey. Toss the roasted veggies with the balsamic dressing and top with fresh basil. Serve immediately.

Here's a fun little story about this salad - one of my friends made this for a potluck and it was a hit! Everyone loved the vibrant and fresh flavors and the juicy, perfectly roasted vegetables. It quickly became one of their most requested dishes.

And finally, let's take a look at the nutritional values. One serving of this salad provides approximately:

198 calories

20g carbohydrates

14g fat

4g protein

27. Marinated Vegetable Salad with Artichokes, Peppers, and Olives

Welcome to the world of flavorful salads! Today, we will be making a scrumptious Mediterranean Marinated Vegetable Salad with Artichokes, Peppers, and Olives. A delightful treat for the taste buds, this salad is sure to leave you wanting more.

For this delicious salad, you will need the following ingredients:

- 1 can of artichoke hearts, drained and halved
- 2 red bell peppers, sliced
- 1 cup of kalamata olives, pitted
- 1 red onion, thinly sliced
- 1/4 cup of balsamic vinegar
- 1/4 cup of olive oil
- Salt and pepper, to taste

This salad can be prepared in just 30 minutes and can serve 4 people. Perfect for a quick and healthy lunch or dinner, you will love the flavors and fresh ingredients in this salad.

Narrative and entertaining instructions (using different wording each time as introduction):

Let's get started! First, preheat your oven to 400°F. Next, place the sliced bell peppers, red onion, and artichoke hearts on a baking sheet. Drizzle with olive oil and season with salt and pepper. Roast in the oven for 20 minutes, or until the vegetables are tender and slightly charred.

In a large bowl, combine the roasted vegetables with the pitted olives. In a small bowl, whisk together the balsamic vinegar and olive oil. Pour the dressing over the salad and mix well. Serve immediately.

This salad is inspired by the sunny beaches of the Mediterranean and is a staple in many homes in the region. Serve it with a crusty piece of bread for a complete meal or as a side dish at your next summer barbecue.

For those who are conscious about what they eat, here is the nutritional information for one serving of this salad:

Calories: 229	Sodium: 844mg	Fiber: 4g
Fat: 19.5g	Carbohydrates: 14g	Protein: 4g

28. Lebanese Lentil Salad with Cilantro and Lemon

Get ready to indulge in a flavor explosion with this scrumptious Lebanese Lentil Salad. A combination of earthy lentils, fresh cilantro, and zesty lemon make this dish a tangy and delicious delight. Perfect for a light lunch or as a side dish to complement any meal, this salad is easy to prepare and packed with nutrients.

Ingredients:

- 1 cup brown or green lentils, rinsed
- 1 large red onion, diced
- 1 cup fresh cilantro leaves, chopped
- 1 lemon, juiced
- 3 tablespoons olive oil
- Salt and pepper, to taste

This dish takes about 30 minutes to prepare and 20 minutes to cook, making it a quick and easy meal that is perfect for busy weeknights. This salad serves 4 to 6 people.

With a little bit of prepping, you'll be diving into this tangy and nutritious Lebanese Lentil Salad in no time! Begin by boiling the lentils in a medium pot of salted water until they are tender, around 25 minutes. While the lentils are cooking, dice the red onion and chop the cilantro leaves. Once the lentils are cooked, drain them and transfer them to a large mixing bowl.

Add the diced red onion, chopped cilantro, lemon juice, olive oil, salt, and pepper to the bowl with the lentils. Mix everything together until the ingredients are evenly distributed and the lentils are fully coated with the lemon dressing.

Serve the lentil salad as a main dish or as a side dish to accompany your favorite protein. It's a delicious and healthy option for those looking to add a burst of flavor to their meals.

This Lebanese Lentil Salad is a staple in Mediterranean cuisine and is often served at family gatherings and special occasions. It's a simple yet delicious dish that's perfect for sharing with loved ones.

Nutritional values per serving:

Calories: 256

Saturated fat: 1.5g

Fiber: 11g

Fat: 11g

Carbohydrates: 32g

Protein: 12

29. Farro Salad with Arugula, Cherry Tomatoes, and Feta

Once upon a time, in a magical land of delicious food, there lived a Farro Salad with Arugula, Cherry Tomatoes, and Feta. This dish was famous for its bright and fresh flavors, the perfect combination of crunchy, juicy and creamy textures, and a healthy twist.

To create this magnificent salad, you'll need the following ingredients:

- 1 cup farro
- 2 cups of water
- 2 cups of arugula
- 1 cup cherry tomatoes, halved
- 1/2 cup crumbled feta cheese
- 2 tablespoons olive oil
- 2 tablespoons balsamic vinegar
- Salt and pepper, to taste

To prepare this dish, you'll need to set aside around 15 minutes for preparation and 30 minutes of cooking time. And once you're done, you'll be able to enjoy this salad as a main course or side dish, serving 4 people.

First, rinse the farro and add it to a pot of boiling water. Cook for 30 minutes or until tender. Drain the farro and let it cool.

In a large bowl, combine the farro, arugula, cherry tomatoes, and feta cheese. Drizzle with olive oil and balsamic vinegar, then season with salt and pepper. Toss gently to combine.

Now here's the fun part: Serve the salad in a big, beautiful bowl and watch as the feta cheese, cherry tomatoes, and balsamic glaze mingle in perfect harmony. Each bite will be a burst of flavor, a celebration of fresh ingredients, and a reminder of why healthy eating can be so darn delicious.

Nutrition Information per Serving:

Calories: 220

Sodium: 230mg

Protein: 7g

Fat: 13g

Carbohydrates: 21g

Fiber: 4g

30. Mediterranean Quinoa Salad with Roasted Red Pepper and Kalamata Olives

Today, we'll be cooking up a storm with a delicious and nutritious Mediterranean Quinoa Salad. This dish is packed with fresh and flavorful ingredients that will tantalize your taste buds and keep you feeling full and satisfied. So, without further ado, let's get started!

Ingredients:

- 1 cup quinoa, rinsed
- 2 cups water
- 1 roasted red pepper, chopped
- 1/2 cup Kalamata olives, pitted
- 1/4 cup red onion, chopped
- 2 tbsp. lemon juice
- 1 tbsp. olive oil
- Salt and pepper, to taste

Cooking time: 20 minutes

Preparation time: 10 minutes

Servings: 4

Now, let's get down to business and put this beautiful dish together. First, in a medium saucepan, bring the quinoa and water to a boil. Reduce heat to low, cover, and simmer for about 20 minutes or until the quinoa is tender and the water is absorbed. Fluff with a fork and set aside to cool.

In a large bowl, mix together the cooled quinoa, roasted red pepper, Kalamata olives, red onion, lemon juice, and olive oil. Season with salt and pepper to taste.

And now, the moment we've all been waiting for. It's time to dig in and enjoy this delicious salad! Serve it up with a side of crusty bread or crackers and a glass of crisp white wine. Trust me, this is one meal you won't forget!

Nutrition per serving:

Calories: 276	Cholesterol: 0mg	Fiber: 4g
Fat: 14g	Sodium: 634mg	Sugar: 2g
Saturated Fat: 2g	Carbohydrates: 32g	Protein: 7g

Now, that was a fun and tasty ride, wasn't it? I hope you enjoyed this Mediterranean Quinoa Salad as much as I did. If you're looking for a healthy and flavorful meal that's perfect for any time of the day, this dish is a winner. Until next time, happy cooking!

Meat

31. Grilled Lamb Chops with Rosemary and Garlic

Get ready for a flavor explosion! Today, we're cooking up some juicy and succulent Grilled Lamb Chops with Rosemary and Garlic. This dish is sure to impress your dinner guests and leave them asking for seconds. Let's get started!

Here's what you'll need:

- 4 lamb chops
- 2 tablespoons fresh rosemary, chopped
- 4 cloves of garlic, minced
- Salt and pepper, to taste
- 2 tablespoons of olive oil

This dish takes 15 minutes to cook and makes 4 servings.

First, let's get our ingredients ready. Chop up the rosemary and mince the garlic.

In a small bowl, mix together the rosemary, garlic, salt, pepper, and olive oil. Rub the mixture all over the lamb chops.

Let the lamb chops marinate in the mixture for at least 30 minutes, or up to overnight for an extra boost of flavor.

When you're ready to cook, preheat your grill to high heat. Place the lamb chops on the grill and cook for 3-4 minutes on each side, or until they reach an internal temperature of 145°F.

And there you have it! A delicious and flavorful dish of Grilled Lamb Chops with Rosemary and Garlic. Serve it with a side of your choice, and enjoy the symphony of flavors in your mouth! Bon appétit!

Did you know that the Romans were huge fans of lamb? In fact, they considered it a symbol of wealth and status. So, go ahead and treat yourself like a Roman emperor and dig into these delectable Grilled Lamb Chops with Rosemary and Garlic!

Nutritional Values:

Calories: 314

Cholesterol: 83mg

Protein: 20g

Fat: 26g

Sodium: 144mg

Saturated Fat: 9g

Carbohydrates: 1g

32. Slow-Cooked Beef Shanks with Red Wine and Thyme

Ladies and Gentlemen, it's time to upgrade your meat game! If you're looking for a recipe that'll make your taste buds dance, this slow-cooked beef shanks with red wine and thyme is the one for you!

Ingredients:

- 4 large beef shanks
- 1 bottle of full-bodied red wine
- 6 cloves of garlic
- 4 sprigs of thyme
- Salt and pepper to taste
- 3 tablespoons of olive oil
- 1 large onion, chopped
- 2 carrots, chopped
- 2 celery stalks, chopped
- 4 cups of beef stock

You'll have to spend about 6 hours cooking these beef shanks, but don't worry, the result will be worth it! As for the preparation time, it won't take you more than 30 minutes. And the best part? You'll be serving 8 generous portions of this deliciousness!

First things first, season the beef shanks with salt and pepper, then brown them in a hot pan with olive oil. After that, transfer them to a slow cooker.

In the same pan, add the chopped onion, carrots, and celery, and cook until they're soft and tender.

Next, add the garlic and cook for another minute. Pour in the red wine and let it reduce for about 5 minutes.

Pour the mixture over the beef shanks in the slow cooker and add the beef stock and thyme.

Turn on the slow cooker and let the magic happen! The beef shanks will be tender and juicy after 6 hours of cooking.

Serve the shanks with mashed potatoes, and enjoy the symphony of flavors in your mouth!

Do you know the saying 'Patience is a virtue'? Well, it's especially true when it comes to slow-cooking! So, pour yourself a glass of red wine, relax, and let the slow cooker do its job. Trust us, you'll thank us later!

Nutritional Values (Serving size: 1 portion 4 oz)

Calories: 365	Protein: 34g	Fiber: 1g
Fat: 21g	Carbohydrates: 5g	Cholesterol: 113mg
Saturated fat: 8g	Sugar: 2g	Sodium: 569mg.

33. Rack of Pork with a Honey and Mustard Glaze

Pork lovers, get ready for a flavor explosion with this mouth-watering Rack of Pork with Honey and Mustard Glaze. Imagine tender and juicy pork smothered in a sweet and tangy sauce, all coming together for the ultimate taste experience. This dish is sure to impress your dinner guests and leave them asking for seconds.

You will need:

- 1 (8-rib) rack of pork, trimmed and patted dry
- Salt and pepper
- 2 tablespoons Dijon mustard
- 3 tablespoons honey
- 1 tablespoon olive oil
- 2 cloves garlic, minced
- 2 sprigs of fresh thyme
- 1/4 cup red wine

This recipe requires 30 minutes active time and 2 hours slow-cook time. It serves 4 people.

Are you ready to get your chef on? Let's start by preheating the oven to 350°F. Season the pork with salt and pepper on both sides and place it in a roasting pan.

In a mixing bowl, whisk together the mustard and honey until well combined. Heat the olive oil in a small saucepan over medium heat and add the minced garlic and fresh thyme. Cook until fragrant, about 1 minute. Add the honey and mustard mixture and red wine to the saucepan and stir to combine. Let the sauce simmer for 5 minutes until it has reduced and thickened slightly.

Next, we're going to brush the glaze over the top of the pork. Make sure to cover every inch of the pork with the sweet and tangy sauce.

Pop the pork in the oven and slow-cook for 2 hours, or until the internal temperature reaches 145°F. Remove from the oven and let it rest for 10 minutes before slicing and serving.

Serve the Rack of Pork with a Honey and Mustard Glaze with your favorite sides and enjoy the ultimate taste experience.

This recipe is a crowd-pleaser and is perfect for special occasions, or just because you feel like treating yourself. You can never go wrong with a good old rack of pork, especially when it's smothered in a honey and mustard glaze. Just remember to have plenty of napkins on hand, because things are about to get messy."

Nutrition values (per serving):

Calories: 551	Cholesterol: 156mg	Fiber: 0g
Fat: 35g	Sodium: 654mg	Sugar: 18g
Saturated Fat: 12g	Carbohydrates: 20g	Protein: 44g

34. ~~Lovely Pork Medallions~~ *Beef & Eggplant Casserole* (handwritten)

Beef and Eggplant Casserole with Tomatoes and Herbs" as "Alpha" Structure:

Greetings, my dear foodies! Are you tired of the same old beef casseroles? Well, buckle up because this recipe is going to take you on a culinary journey to the Mediterranean with its succulent beef and juicy eggplants simmered in a spicy tomato sauce.

Gather These Marvelous Ingredients for 4 servings:

- 1 pound ground beef
- 2 large eggplants, sliced
- 1 can of crushed tomatoes
- 2 cloves of garlic, minced
- 1 tsp dried basil
- 1 tsp dried oregano
- 1 tsp dried thyme
- Salt and pepper, to taste

The slow-paced simmering of the ingredients is what makes this casserole so flavorful and juicy. Allow around 2 hours and 30 minutes to fully enjoy the richness of this delightful dish. Before you begin, take some time to chop and slice the ingredients, it'll take about 30 minutes. Trust us, the end result will be worth it!

Now, let's get cooking! First, you want to start by browning the ground beef in a large skillet over medium heat. Make sure to season it with salt and pepper for added flavor. Once it's browned, set it aside.

Next, grab your trusty eggplants and slice them into rounds. In the same skillet, add a touch of oil and cook the eggplant until they're golden brown on both sides. Set them aside with the beef.

In the meantime, let's create the tomato sauce. In a saucepan, heat up the crushed tomatoes, minced garlic, and dried herbs. Let it simmer for a few minutes, and then add the browned beef and eggplant.

Once everything is combined, transfer the casserole to a 9x13 inch baking dish. Cover with foil and bake in a preheated 375°F oven for 30 minutes.

This casserole always reminds me of my grandmother's cooking. She used to make it for special occasions and everyone would fight over the last serving. It's one of those dishes that brings the family together and creates lasting memories.

Nutritional Values (per serving):

Calories: 348	Carbohydrates: 19.1g	Fiber: 6.7
Fat: 17.8g	Protein: 28.1g	

And there you have it, a delicious and hearty "Beef and Eggplant Casserole with Tomatoes and Herbs." Perfect for a family dinner or a cozy night in. Enjoy!

35. Stuffed Bell Peppers with Ground Beef and Rice

Once upon a time, there was a craving for a hearty, warm and comforting dinner. And so, the dish of Stuffed Bell Peppers was born! This dish is a perfect balance of tender bell peppers filled to the brim with juicy and flavorful ground beef and fluffy, nutty rice. It's the ultimate comfort food and is sure to be a crowd-pleaser.

Here's what you'll need:

- 4 large bell peppers, sliced in half and seeded
- 1 lb. ground beef
- 1 cup cooked rice
- 1 large onion, chopped
- 2 cloves of garlic, minced
- 1 can of diced tomatoes
- 1 tbsp. tomato paste
- 1 tsp. dried basil
- 1 tsp. dried oregano
- Salt and pepper, to taste
- 1 cup shredded mozzarella cheese

Start to finish, this delicious dish will take you around 45 minutes, with 25 minutes of preparation time and 20 minutes of cooking time. It will serve 4-6 people.

To get started, preheat your oven to 375°F. In a large skillet, cook the ground beef over medium heat until browned and crumbled. Drain off any excess grease. Add the chopped onions, minced garlic, diced tomatoes, tomato paste, dried basil, dried oregano, salt and pepper to the skillet and cook for about 5 minutes, until the onions are translucent and fragrant. Stir in the cooked rice.

Next, spoon the beef and rice mixture into the bell pepper halves. Place the stuffed bell peppers in a 9x13 inch baking dish and sprinkle the shredded mozzarella cheese on top. Bake in the preheated oven for 20 minutes, or until the cheese is melted and bubbly.

Here's an anecdote to make you smile: A little girl once asked her grandmother why they stuff bell peppers. The grandmother replied "Honey, it's because bell peppers are like pockets. They're made to be filled with delicious things!"

And now, for the nutritional information you've been eagerly waiting for:

Calories: 340	Carbohydrates: 20g	Fiber: 3g
Fat: 18g	Protein: 22g	Sodium: 360mg

Dig in and enjoy the taste explosion in your mouth!

36. Braised Beef Short Ribs with Carrots and Parsnips

Are you in the mood for some comforting and lip-smacking beef ribs that are slow-cooked to tender perfection? Well, then buckle up, because this recipe is going to take you on a flavor journey!

For this scrumptious dish, you'll need:

- 4 pounds of beef short ribs
- 4 large carrots, peeled and chopped into chunks
- 4 large parsnips, peeled and chopped into chunks
- 1 large onion, chopped
- 3 cloves of garlic, minced
- 2 cups of beef broth
- 1 cup of red wine
- 2 tablespoons of tomato paste
- 1 teaspoon of dried thyme
- Salt and pepper to taste
- 2 tablespoons of olive oil

First, let's prep the ingredients. This should take you around 15 minutes. Then, we'll get to the fun part - cooking! The cooking time for these delicious beef short ribs is around 3 hours. And when they're ready, they'll serve 6 to 8 people.

In a large Dutch oven or a heavy-bottomed pot, heat the olive oil over medium heat. Add the chopped onions and cook until they're soft and translucent, around 5 minutes. Add the minced garlic and cook for another minute. Then, add the tomato paste and cook for another minute until it's fragrant.

Add the beef broth, red wine, thyme, salt, and pepper to the pot. Stir well. Add the beef short ribs and make sure they're covered by the liquid. Bring the mixture to a simmer, then reduce the heat to low, cover the pot, and let it simmer for 2 to 3 hours, or until the beef is tender.

Stir in the chopped carrots and parsnips into the pot and let them cook for another 20 to 30 minutes, or until they're tender. Serve the beef short ribs with the vegetables, and don't forget to spoon some of the sauce over them!

This dish is perfect for a cozy night in or for a special occasion with family and friends. And if you're feeling adventurous, try serving it with mashed potatoes or crusty bread to soak up all that delicious sauce.

An Anecdote:

Did you know that parsnips were a popular food among ancient Romans? They believed that parsnips had healing powers and would often eat them for medicinal purposes. Who knew that this humble root vegetable would still be enjoyed over 2000 years later?

Nutritional Values (per serving):

Calories: 710

Cholesterol: 210mg

Fiber: 4g

Fat: 43g

Sodium: 870mg

Sugar: 8g

Saturated Fat: 17g

Carbohydrates: 16g

Protein: 57g

37. Beef Kofta Skewers with Yogurt and Cucumber Sauce

Welcome to the land of skewers and sauces! Today, we're whipping up a tantalizing treat for your taste buds - Beef Kofta Skewers with Yogurt and Cucumber Sauce. Get your grilling game on and let's get started!

First things first, let's gather the ingredients for this delicious dish. You'll need:

- 500g minced beef
- 1 medium onion, grated
- 2 garlic cloves, minced
- 1 teaspoon ground cumin
- 1 teaspoon ground coriander
- 1 teaspoon paprika
- Salt and pepper, to taste
- Skewers (if using wooden skewers, soak in water for 30 minutes to prevent burning)
- 1 cup plain yogurt
- 1/2 cucumber, peeled and grated
- 1 tablespoon lemon juice
- Salt, to taste

Now that we have all the ingredients in place, let's move on to the cooking time. This dish will take approximately 30 minutes to cook and 15 minutes to prepare. Serve it to 4 hungry stomachs, or 2 really really hungry ones!

Let's start by preparing the koftas. In a large bowl, mix together the minced beef, grated onion, minced garlic, cumin, coriander, paprika, salt and pepper. Shape into 8 sausage-like portions and thread onto skewers.

Grill the kofta skewers over medium-high heat for about 10 minutes on each side, or until fully cooked.

While the koftas are cooking, let's prepare the sauce. In a medium bowl, mix together the yogurt, grated cucumber, lemon juice and salt. Serve alongside the kofta skewers.

An interesting fact about this dish, in the Middle Eastern countries it's common to serve the kofta skewers with a spicy tomato sauce, but the cool and refreshing cucumber sauce is a perfect contrast to the spiced meat.

And finally, the moment we've all been waiting for - the nutritional values. One serving of this delicious dish contains approximately:

230 calories   23g protein

15g fat   4g carbohydrates

Satisfy your cravings and dig in! Enjoy your Beef Kofta Skewers with Yogurt and Cucumber Sauce.

38. Grilled Flank Steak with Chimichurri Sauce

Fire up the grill, grab your steak and get ready for a mouthwatering adventure! This Grilled Flank Steak with Chimichurri Sauce is like a fiesta in your mouth, it's time to dig in and let the flavor explosion begin!"

For this recipe, you'll need a little something for the steak and a little something for the sauce. Let's start with the steak ingredients:

- 1 lb flank steak
- 2 teaspoons of garlic powder
- 1 teaspoon of salt
- 1 teaspoon of black pepper

And now for the sauce, the cherry on top of this steak sundae:

- 1 cup of fresh parsley
- 1/2 cup of fresh cilantro
- 3 cloves of garlic
- 1/2 teaspoon of dried oregano
- 1/2 teaspoon of red pepper flakes
- 1/2 teaspoon of salt
- 1/4 cup of red wine vinegar
- 1/2 cup of extra virgin olive oil

This Grilled Flank Steak is quick and easy, and it will take you no time to get it on the table. Cooking time is around 10-12 minutes, preparation time is 15 minutes, and it makes 4 servings.

Take the flank steak out of the fridge and let it sit for about 15 minutes. During that time, let's make the chimichurri sauce. Blend all the ingredients in a food processor until smooth. Reserve half of the sauce for serving.

Season the steak with garlic powder, salt, and pepper. Place the steak on a hot grill and cook for 5 minutes on each side or until it reaches your desired level of doneness.

Take the steak off the grill and let it rest for about 5 minutes. Slice the steak against the grain and serve with the remaining chimichurri sauce.

Anecdote:

This Grilled Flank Steak with Chimichurri Sauce is perfect for those hot summer nights when you want to enjoy a delicious meal without spending hours in the kitchen. It's easy, quick, and guaranteed to impress your guests!"

For all those health-conscious foodies out there, here's what you've been waiting for! A single serving of Grilled Flank Steak with Chimichurri Sauce provides:

324 calories

23g of fat

26g of protein

2g of carbohydrates

Bon Appétit!

39. Slow-Cooked Bolognese Sauce with Ground Beef and Tomatoes

Gather around foodie friends, it's time to learn how to make a classic Italian dish with a twist! Introducing Slow-Cooked Bolognese Sauce with Ground Beef and Tomatoes - a recipe so simple, yet so delicious, it will make you want to twirl spaghetti around your fork all day long.

And now, for the stars of the show, the ingredients! Get your aprons ready, it's time to go shopping. We'll need:

- 1 lb. ground beef
- 1 onion, diced
- 2 cloves of garlic, minced
- 2 carrots, diced
- 2 celery stalks, diced
- 1 (28 oz) can of crushed tomatoes
- 1/2 cup of red wine
- Salt
- Pepper
- 2 tablespoons of olive oil
- A handful of fresh basil leaves

This recipe makes enough sauce for about 6-8 portions, so gather the family and dig in!

You must be thinking, what makes this Bolognese Sauce so special? The secret ingredient is time, my friend, we'll need about 4 hours of your time. The slow cooking process allows all the flavors to blend together and creates a rich, hearty sauce that's sure to become your new favorite.

The prep time for this recipe is a mere 15 minutes, which includes dicing and mincing your veggies. Once that's done, heat up a large pot with olive oil and add the ground beef. Cook the beef until it's browned and set it aside. In the same pot, add the onion, garlic, carrots, and celery. Cook until they're soft and fragrant, about 10 minutes.

Now, pour in the red wine, let it simmer for 2-3 minutes, then add the canned tomatoes and the browned beef. Stir everything together, bring to a boil, then reduce the heat to low. Cover the pot and let the sauce simmer for 2-3 hours.

During this time, take a break and go do something fun! Maybe read a book, take a nap, or call a friend. When you return, the aroma of the Bolognese Sauce will fill your home, making your mouth water in anticipation.

Just before serving, season the sauce with salt and pepper to taste and add a handful of fresh basil leaves. Serve it over your favorite pasta and enjoy!

And now, for a little story to accompany this amazing dish. Did you know that Bolognese Sauce originated in the northern Italian city of Bologna? It's said that the sauce was created to feed the many hungry students at the local university. The professors loved it so much, they began to serve it to their guests. And, thus, the famous Bolognese Sauce was born!

If you're counting, here are the nutritional values for one serving of this dish:

Cal: 394

Carbs: 20g

Fat: 23g

Protein: 27g

Buon Appetito!

40. Mediterranean Beef and Bulgur Wheat Salad with Herbs and Feta

Step right up and prepare your taste buds for a flavor explosion! Today, we're whipping up a Mediterranean Beef and Bulgur Wheat Salad that'll have your mouth watering and your belly full of deliciousness.

To start, you'll need the following ingredients:

- 1 lb. of sirloin steak, sliced into thin strips
- 1 cup of bulgur wheat
- 1 cup of cherry tomatoes, halved
- 1 cup of cucumber, diced
- 1/2 cup of crumbled feta cheese
- 1/4 cup of parsley, chopped
- 1/4 cup of mint, chopped
- 1/4 cup of lemon juice
- 2 tablespoons of olive oil
- Salt and pepper to taste

Now let's get started! It'll take you around 20 minutes to prepare and another 15 minutes to cook this scrumptious salad. Trust us, it's worth every second. And don't worry, you'll only need to serve 4 hungry mouths!

First, we'll cook the bulgur wheat according to the package instructions. While that's cooking, heat a large skillet over medium-high heat and add in the sliced sirloin steak. Season with salt and pepper and cook until browned, about 5 minutes.

Next, in a large bowl, mix together the cooked bulgur wheat, cherry tomatoes, cucumber, feta cheese, parsley, mint, lemon juice, and olive oil. Season with salt and pepper to taste.

Now for the fun part! Arrange the steak on top of the bulgur wheat mixture and you're all set! Serve this salad at your next outdoor picnic or summer barbeque and watch as it quickly becomes a crowd favorite.

And let me tell you a little secret... this salad is not just delicious, it's healthy too!

Here's a breakdown of the nutrients you'll be devouring:

Total fat: 15 g	Sodium: 250 mg	Dietary fiber: 7 g
Cholesterol: 40 mg	Total carbohydrate: 28 g	Protein: 28 g

Enjoy your Mediterranean Beef and Bulgur Wheat Salad with Herbs and Feta! It's a savory explosion of flavors that'll keep you coming back for seconds...or maybe even thirds.

Poultry

41. Grilled Turkey Kebabs

Ladies and Gentlemen, gather 'round for a taste explosion like no other! Introducing the ultimate crowd-pleaser - Grilled Turkey Kebabs! A perfect balance of juicy, tender turkey, and a flavorful medley of seasonings and spices. Before we dive into the ingredients, let's just take a moment to appreciate the versatility of our main man - the turkey. He's not just for Thanksgiving, you know? He's got moves, he's got style, and he's ready to take center stage on your grill.

And now, onto the star ingredients! You will need:

- 1 lb ground turkey
- 1 red bell pepper, diced
- 1 yellow onion, diced
- 8 cherry tomatoes
- 1/4 cup olive oil
- 2 cloves of garlic, minced
- 2 tbsp freshly squeezed lemon juice
- 1 tbsp dried oregano
- 1 tsp paprika
- 1 tsp salt
- 1/2 tsp black pepper
- 8 skewers

Fire up the grill and let's get cooking! This recipe will take you around 30 minutes to prepare and 10-15 minutes to cook. It'll feed 4 hungry bellies, so feel free to double up if you're hosting a BBQ bash.

First, let's make the marinade. In a bowl, whisk together the olive oil, lemon juice, garlic, oregano, paprika, salt, and pepper. Add the ground turkey to the bowl and mix well to combine. Then, divide the turkey mixture into 8 equal portions and shape each portion around a skewer. Alternating with the red bell pepper, yellow onion, and cherry tomatoes.

Now, let's get grilling! Place the kebabs on a preheated grill over medium-high heat. Cook for 10-15 minutes, turning occasionally, until the turkey is fully cooked through and the vegetables are slightly charred.

And there you have it, folks! Grilled Turkey Kebabs that are juicy, tender, and full of flavor. I remember my grandfather used to make these for our family barbecues, and they always disappeared in minutes! People would start fighting over the last skewer, it was wild! He had a secret ingredient that he never revealed, but I'm convinced it was just love.

Nutrition per serving:

320 calories	36g protein	6g sugar
22g fat	11g carbohydrates	320mg sodium
4g saturated fat	2g fiber	

42. Chicken Shawarma with Tabbouleh

When it comes to serving up a delicious and satisfying meal, it doesn't get much better than chicken shawarma. And to take things to the next level, we've paired it with a side of tangy and fresh tabbouleh. This recipe will take you on a culinary journey to the Mediterranean and back!

So, let's gather our ingredients and get started. You will need:

- 1 large boneless, skinless chicken breast, sliced into thin strips
- 2 teaspoons ground cumin
- 2 teaspoons ground coriander
- 1 teaspoon ground turmeric
- 1 teaspoon paprika
- 1/2 teaspoon cayenne pepper
- Salt and pepper, to taste
- 3 tablespoons olive oil
- 2 cloves of garlic, minced
- 4 whole wheat pita breads
- 1 cup cherry tomatoes, halved
- 1 English cucumber, diced
- 1/2 cup fresh parsley leaves, chopped
- 1/2 cup fresh mint leaves, chopped
- 1/2 lemon, juiced
- 2 tablespoons olive oil
- 1 cup bulgur wheat, cooked according to package directions
- 1/2 cup crumbled feta cheese
- Alright, let's get to work!

First things first, let's get our chicken marinade together. In a small bowl, mix together the cumin, coriander, turmeric, paprika, cayenne, salt, pepper, and olive oil. Rub this mixture all over the chicken strips and let them marinate for at least 30 minutes, or up to 24 hours if you have the time.

Now it's time to get cooking! Heat a large skillet over medium-high heat and add the chicken. Cook for about 8-10 minutes, or until the chicken is cooked through and nicely browned. While the chicken is cooking, let's get our tabbouleh together. In a large bowl, mix together the cherry tomatoes, cucumber, parsley, mint, lemon juice, and olive oil. Stir in the cooked bulgur wheat and feta cheese, and set aside.

Once the chicken is cooked, warm the pita breads in the oven or on the stove. To assemble your shawarma, place a pita bread on a plate, top with the chicken, and then spoon on the tabbouleh. Fold the pita over and enjoy!

I remember the first time I tried chicken shawarma in a street market in Istanbul. It was love at first bite! The juicy, tender chicken combined with the fresh, bright flavors of the tabbouleh was a match made in heaven. I knew I had to recreate this delicious dish in my own kitchen and share it with my loved ones.

This dish is not only delicious, but it's also a nutritious choice. Each serving of chicken shawarma with tabbouleh provides roughly:

Calories: 450

Cholesterol: 60 mg

Dietary Fiber: 8 g

Total Fat: 19 g

Sodium: 480 mg

Protein: 26 g

Saturated Fat: 4 g

Total Carbohydrates: 46 g

So there you have it, a fun and flavorful recipe for chicken shawarma with tabbouleh that's sure to be a hit with your taste buds and your waistline!

43. Mediterranean Roasted Chicken

Ah, the Mediterranean Roasted Chicken, a dish fit for royalty! Imagine biting into juicy and succulent chicken that's seasoned to perfection, bursting with the flavors of the Mediterranean. I'm getting hungry just thinking about it!

So, what do you need to create this masterpiece? Well, let me give you the rundown of the ingredients you'll need. You'll need to round up some chicken, of course, a lemon, some garlic, and a handful of herbs. Oh, and don't forget the olive oil, that's the key ingredient for any Mediterranean dish. The exact list and quantities of ingredients are listed below.

Here's what you'll need to gather up:

- 1 whole chicken (4 to 5 pounds)
- 1 lemon, cut into wedges
- 8 cloves of garlic, minced
- 4 tablespoons of olive oil
- 2 teaspoons dried oregano
- 1 teaspoon dried thyme
- 1 teaspoon dried rosemary
- Salt and pepper to taste

Now, let's talk about the timing. Roasting a chicken takes a bit of time, so be sure to plan accordingly. The preparation time is about 15 minutes, and the cooking time is 1 hour and 30 minutes. But don't worry, you can sit back, relax and let the oven do the work for you! This recipe makes 4 to 6 servings, perfect for a family dinner or a dinner party with friends.

So, let's get to the fun part - cooking the chicken! Preheat your oven to 400 degrees F. Pat the chicken dry with paper towels and season it generously with salt and pepper, both inside and out. Then, stuff the lemon wedges and garlic inside the cavity of the chicken.

In a small bowl, mix together the olive oil, oregano, thyme, and rosemary. Then, using your hands, rub the mixture all over the chicken, making sure to cover every nook and cranny. Place the chicken in a roasting pan, breast-side up, and pop it in the oven.

Let the chicken roast for 1 hour and 30 minutes, or until the skin is golden brown and crispy and the internal temperature of the chicken reaches 165 degrees F. Baste the chicken every 30 minutes with the juices that have collected in the pan to keep the chicken moist.

Once the chicken is fully roasted, take it out of the oven and let it rest for 10 minutes before carving it into pieces. Serve the chicken with some crusty bread and a green salad on the side, and you're good to go!

Now, for the nutritional values. This dish is packed with protein, iron, and other essential nutrients. Per serving, you'll get:

Calories: 350

Sodium: 130mg

Sugar: 1g

Fat: 22g

Carbohydrates: 6g

Protein: 35g

Cholesterol: 110mg

Fiber: 2g

And finally, a little anecdote to end the recipe. Did you know that in ancient Greece, roasting a whole chicken was a symbol of wealth and prosperity? People would often host large feasts and roast whole chickens to impress their guests. So, next time you serve this dish to your family or friends, you can tell them the story and make them feel like royalty!

44. Chicken Tagine with Apricots and Almonds

Alrighty, let's spice up this recipe for Chicken Tagine with Apricots and Almonds! Tagine, for those of you who don't know, is a traditional North African stew made in a conical-shaped cooking pot. This dish is perfect for those who want to add some excitement to their taste buds and explore new flavors!

Now, before we dive into the ingredients, let's talk about what makes this dish unique. Apricots and almonds are the stars of the show here, but they're not just randomly thrown in. The sweetness of the apricots balances out the savory flavors of the chicken, while the crunchy almonds add a delightful texture. It's like a dance party in your mouth!

For this recipe, you'll need the following:

- 4 skinless, boneless chicken thighs
- 1 large onion, diced
- 4 cloves garlic, minced
- 1 tsp. cumin
- 1 tsp. paprika
- 1 tsp. cinnamon
- 1/2 tsp. ground ginger
- Salt and pepper, to taste
- 1 cup chicken broth
- 1/2 cup dried apricots
- 1/2 cup slivered almonds
- Fresh cilantro, for garnish

Alright, let's get to cooking! First things first, let's talk about timing. This dish will take about 45 minutes to cook, and about 10 minutes to prepare. It serves 4 people, which is perfect for a small family gathering or a cozy night in.

To start, heat a large skillet over medium-high heat. Add the chicken and cook until browned on both sides, about 6 minutes. Remove the chicken from the skillet and set it aside. In the same skillet, add the onion and cook until soft and translucent, about 5 minutes. Add the garlic, cumin, paprika, cinnamon, ginger, salt, and pepper and cook for another minute.

Next, pour in the chicken broth, apricots, and slivered almonds, and stir everything together. Return the chicken to the skillet, making sure it's well coated in the sauce. Reduce the heat to low, cover the skillet, and let everything simmer for about 30 minutes.

Now, this is where the magic happens! The apricots will start to break down, creating a sweet and thick sauce. The almonds will add a crunchy texture, and the chicken will be so tender it'll fall off the bone.

When everything is ready, transfer the chicken and sauce to a serving dish and sprinkle with fresh cilantro. Serve hot with some crusty bread, and enjoy the flavors of North Africa!

And now, for the final touch, let's talk about the nutritional values. One serving of this dish will give you approximately:

220 calories	25g of protein	3g of fiber
7g of fat	16g of carbohydrates	9g of sugar

So, what are you waiting for? Get your hands on those ingredients and get cooking! This Chicken Tagine with Apricots and Almonds is sure to impress your taste buds and leave you with a full belly and a smile on your face.

45. Lemon and Herb Stuffed Turkey Breast

Ready for a zesty, flavorful, and juicy turkey experience? Well buckle up, buttercup, because today we're whipping up a lemon and herb stuffed turkey breast that's sure to tantalize your taste buds and leave you and your dinner guests wanting more.

To make this mouth-watering dish, you'll need to gather the following ingredients:

- 1 (3-4 lb) boneless, skin-on turkey breast
- 1 lemon, zested
- 1/2 cup chopped fresh parsley
- 1/4 cup chopped fresh thyme
- 1/4 cup chopped fresh rosemary
- 2 cloves garlic, minced
- 1/4 cup olive oil
- Salt and pepper, to taste

To make this dish, you'll need to set aside about 10 minutes for preparation and about 1 hour and 15 minutes for cooking. This recipe will yield 4-6 servings.

Now, let's get to the fun part - stuffing this bad boy. In a mixing bowl, combine the lemon zest, parsley, thyme, rosemary, garlic, and olive oil. Season with salt and pepper, to taste. Then, using a sharp knife, make a deep slit lengthwise down the center of the turkey breast, being careful not to cut all the way through. Spread the lemon herb mixture evenly inside the turkey breast, making sure to fill the entire cavity.

With the stuffing complete, it's time to cook. Preheat your oven to 400°F. Place the turkey breast in a roasting pan and roast for about 1 hour and 15 minutes, or until the internal temperature of the turkey reaches 165°F. Remove from the oven and let rest for 10 minutes before slicing.

Now, here's a little funny story. One time, I stuffed a turkey with so much lemon and herbs that when I cut into it, the stuffing exploded like a flavor bomb all over my kitchen. But let's not make that mistake today, friends.

Now, let's talk about the nitty gritty. The following are estimated nutritional values for one serving of this dish (based on 6 servings):

Calories: 467	Cholesterol: 193 mg	Fiber: 1 g
Fat: 25 g	Sodium: 328 mg	Sugar: 1 g
Saturated Fat: 5 g	Carbohydrates: 4 g	Protein: 57 g

There you have it, folks! A juicy and flavorful lemon and herb stuffed turkey breast that's sure to be the star of any dinner party

46. Chicken Souvlaki

Let's embark on a culinary journey to Greece with "Chicken Souvlaki"! This dish is a staple in the Greek cuisine and is loved for its succulent chicken marinated in herbs and spices, grilled to perfection, and served with a side of warm pita bread. This dish will take your taste buds on a vacation and make you feel like you're dining on the sunny beaches of Santorini.

Before we dive into the list of ingredients, let's have a little fun! Imagine yourself shopping at a bustling Greek market, haggling with the vendors over the freshest produce and herbs. But wait, where's the chicken? Oh, look, there it is! Hanging on a hook, just waiting to be taken home and transformed into the most delicious souvlaki.

Ingredients:

- 1 lb boneless, skinless chicken breasts, cut into 1 1/2 inch pieces
- 1/4 cup olive oil
- 2 lemons, juiced
- 4 garlic cloves, minced
- 2 tbsp dried oregano
- 1 tsp salt
- 1 tsp black pepper
- 4 skewers
- 4 pita breads
- 1 small red onion, sliced
- 1 small tomato, diced
- 1/2 cucumber, diced
- 1/4 cup fresh parsley, chopped

Cooking time: 10-15 minutes   Preparation time: 30 minutes (plus marinating time)   Servings: 4

Now, let's get to the fun part - grilling the chicken! In a large bowl, mix together the olive oil, lemon juice, garlic, oregano, salt, and pepper. Add the chicken and let marinate for at least 30 minutes (or up to 4 hours for maximum flavor).

Next, grab your skewers and thread the chicken onto them, alternating with pieces of onion. Fire up the grill and place the skewers on it, cooking for 10-15 minutes, or until the chicken is cooked through.

While the chicken is grilling, warm up the pita bread on the grill and mix together the tomato, cucumber, and parsley to make a quick and fresh tzatziki-style sauce.

When the chicken is done, remove it from the grill and place it inside the warm pita bread. Top with the tzatziki-style sauce, wrap it up, and enjoy!

When I first tried souvlaki, I was skeptical. I mean, how good could grilled chicken on a stick really be? But one bite and I was hooked! The juicy chicken, the burst of lemon and herbs, and the soft, warm pita bread... it was love at first bite. I now make it a tradition to have souvlaki every summer, grilling up a big batch for my friends and family. It's always a hit!

Nutritional Values per Serving:

Calories: 580

Cholesterol: 95mg

Fiber: 3g

Fat: 26g

Sodium: 910mg

Sugar: 5g

Saturated Fat: 5g

Carbohydrates: 46g

Protein: 44g

47. Mediterranean Chicken Salad

Ready to add some Mediterranean zest to your meal game? Look no further than this vibrant and flavorful Mediterranean Chicken Salad!

Let's start with the ingredients, shall we? To assemble this dish, you'll need:

- 4 boneless chicken breasts, cooked and diced
- 2 heads of romaine lettuce, chopped
- 1 cup cherry tomatoes, halved
- 1 cup kalamata olives, pitted
- 1/2 cup red onion, diced
- 1/2 cup feta cheese, crumbled
- 1/4 cup extra-virgin olive oil
- 2 tablespoons red wine vinegar
- 2 tablespoons lemon juice
- 1 tablespoon Dijon mustard
- Salt and pepper, to taste

Now, let's get cooking! Preparation time for this dish is a breezy 15 minutes, with a cooking time of 10 minutes. And voila! In no time, you'll be able to serve 4-6 of your lucky friends and family.

To get started, whisk together the olive oil, red wine vinegar, lemon juice, Dijon mustard, salt and pepper in a large bowl. Then, add in the chicken, romaine lettuce, cherry tomatoes, kalamata olives, red onion, and feta cheese. Toss everything together until well combined and evenly coated in the dressing.

An old Mediterranean saying goes, "A salad is only as good as its dressing." And with this Mediterranean Chicken Salad, you'll be the king or queen of the dressing game! The tangy lemon and vinegar meld beautifully with the creamy mustard, creating a harmony of flavors that will have your taste buds singing.

To add a little more excitement to your meal, why not turn it into a picnic? Grab a blanket, some friends, and head to your nearest park. Sit back, relax and enjoy your delicious Mediterranean Chicken Salad in the great outdoors.

And finally, for all you nutrition nuts out there, here's the skinny on this dish:

Calories: 445	Cholesterol: 98 mg	Total Carbohydrates: 9 g
Total Fat: 32 g	Sodium: 583 mg	Protein: 33 g

Bon appétit!

48. Chicken and Olive Tapenade

Ladies and Gentlemen, are you ready for a journey through the streets of Mediterranean? Then buckle up and get ready to taste the most delicious and flavorful tapenade that you've ever had! I'm talking about Chicken and Olive Tapenade that is packed with so much flavor, it's bound to leave you asking for more. Let's get started with the ingredients.

The ingredients, my friends, are like a parade of flavors marching towards your taste buds! For this scrumptious tapenade, you'll need:

- 4 boneless, skinless chicken breasts (about 1 1/2 pounds)
- Salt and freshly ground black pepper
- 2 tablespoons olive oil
- 1 cup pitted kalamata olives
- 1/4 cup capers, drained
- 2 garlic cloves, minced
- 2 tablespoons freshly squeezed lemon juice
- 1/4 cup chopped fresh flat-leaf parsley
- Crusty bread, for serving

With these ingredients, your tapenade is sure to be a hit at the dinner table!

Now that we have the ingredients ready, it's time to prepare the tapenade. Let me tell you, this tapenade is not just a recipe, it's an experience! Cooking time for this beauty is about 15 minutes and preparation time is about 10 minutes. You can serve 4 people with this recipe.

To start, season the chicken breasts with salt and pepper. In a large skillet, heat the olive oil over medium heat. Add the chicken to the skillet and cook until browned and cooked through, about 6 minutes per side. Remove the chicken from the skillet and let it cool.

While the chicken is cooling, in a food processor, combine the olives, capers, garlic, lemon juice, and parsley. Pulse until the mixture is finely chopped.

Once the chicken has cooled, slice it into thin strips. Serve the chicken with the olive tapenade and crusty bread. It's the perfect dish for a Mediterranean-style dinner party!

Let me tell you a little anecdote about this dish. This recipe was inspired by a trip to the Mediterranean where I had the opportunity to taste this tapenade for the first time. It was love at first bite and I knew that I had to recreate this dish back home. And that's how this recipe was born!

Now, let's talk about the nutritional values of this dish. This tapenade is a good source of protein, healthy fats, and fiber.

Per serving:

Calories: 340	Cholesterol: 93 mg	Dietary Fiber: 2 g
Total Fat: 21 g	Sodium: 1040 mg	Sugar: 1 g
Saturated Fat: 4 g	Total Carbohydrates: 6 g	Protein: 34 g

So, go ahead and try this delicious and healthy Chicken and Olive Tapenade recipe!

49. Chicken and Mushroom Risotto

Are you ready to become a master of the risotto game? Well buckle up, buttercup, because today we're making a classic and comforting dish with a little twist - Chicken and Mushroom Risotto!

First things first, let's gather the ingredients for our delicious masterpiece. You'll need:

- 1 lb boneless, skinless chicken breast, cut into 1-inch pieces
- 8 oz mushrooms, sliced
- 1 onion, finely chopped
- 2 garlic cloves, minced
- 1 cup arborio rice
- 4 cups chicken broth
- 1 cup white wine
- 1/2 cup grated Parmesan cheese
- 2 tbsp olive oil
- 2 tbsp butter
- Salt and pepper, to taste

Now that we've got all our ingredients ready to go, let's get to cooking! This delightful dish will take approximately 35 minutes to cook and 10 minutes to prep. It will serve 4-6 people, so invite your friends and family over to enjoy this mouth-watering meal.

We'll start by heating the olive oil in a large saucepan over medium heat. Add the chicken pieces and cook until browned on all sides. Remove the chicken from the pan and set aside. In the same pan, add the mushrooms, onion, and garlic. Cook until the vegetables are tender and the mushrooms have released their moisture. Remove the vegetables from the pan and set aside with the chicken.

Next, add the arborio rice to the pan and stir continuously until the rice is coated with the oil and has turned a light golden color. Pour in the white wine and continue to stir until the wine has been absorbed by the rice.

Start adding the chicken broth, one ladleful at a time, stirring continuously until each addition has been absorbed before adding the next. Continue this process until the rice is tender but still firm to the bite. This should take about 20-25 minutes.

Once the rice is cooked, add the chicken, mushrooms, and vegetables back to the pan and stir until heated through. Stir in the Parmesan cheese and butter until melted and well combined.

And that's it! A simple and scrumptious dish that's sure to please even the pickiest of eaters. But don't just take my word for it, give it a try and see for yourself.

Here's a little anecdote to spice things up - a man once told me that the secret to a good risotto is to add a splash of love and a pinch of laughter. So, don't forget to add both of these ingredients to your dish and you'll have the best risotto in town.

Last but not least, let's take a look at the nutritional values for our Chicken and Mushroom Risotto:

Calories: 550

Sodium: 870mg

Protein: 40g

Fat: 24g

Carbohydrates: 39g

Fiber: 2g

And there you have it! A hearty and healthy meal that's sure to please everyone at the dinner table. Happy cooking!

50. Moroccan Chicken with Preserved Lemons

Feast your eyes, folks, on a culinary journey to the sun-kissed land of Morocco! Today, we're whipping up a flavorful, aromatic and hearty dish that's guaranteed to leave you full, satisfied and licking your fingers. Presenting, the one, the only, Moroccan Chicken with Preserved Lemons!

First things first, let's gather all the magical ingredients that'll make this dish truly unforgettable. You'll need the following:

- 4 boneless, skinless chicken breasts
- 1/4 cup olive oil
- 1 large onion, chopped
- 4 cloves of garlic, minced
- 1 teaspoon paprika
- 1 teaspoon cumin
- 1 teaspoon coriander
- 1 teaspoon cinnamon
- 1/2 teaspoon cayenne pepper
- 1/2 cup chicken broth
- 1/2 cup white wine
- 4 preserved lemons, chopped
- Salt and pepper to taste
- 1 cup chopped cilantro for garnish

And with that, we're ready to start cooking!

The cooking time for this savory delight is around 45 minutes, but the preparation time is just 15 minutes. This dish will be a hit at any gathering and will serve about 4 people.

So, let's start by heating the olive oil in a large skillet over medium heat. Add the onion and garlic and cook until soft and fragrant. Then, add the chicken and cook until browned on both sides. Sprinkle the paprika, cumin, coriander, cinnamon, and cayenne pepper over the chicken and cook for 1-2 minutes more.

Pour in the chicken broth and white wine and bring the mixture to a boil. Reduce the heat to low and cover the skillet. Let it simmer for 20-25 minutes, or until the chicken is cooked through. Stir in the chopped preserved lemons and cilantro and season with salt and pepper to taste.

And just like that, your Moroccan Chicken with Preserved Lemons is ready to be devoured! Serve it with a side of couscous or rice for a truly authentic dining experience.

A fun fact about preserved lemons: They were used by ancient Moroccans to add a tangy, salty flavor to their dishes. Today, they're a staple in Moroccan cuisine and are widely used in various recipes to add a unique and exotic touch.

Now for the moment you've all been waiting for, the Nutritional values per serving (4 servings in total):

Calories: 458

Sodium: 883mg

Fiber: 4g

Fat: 25g

Carbohydrates: 12g

Protein: 42g

So, there you have it folks! A flavorful and nutritious dish that's sure to leave you feeling satisfied. Happy cooking!

Seafood

51. Grilled Mediterranean Sea Bass with Olive Tapenade and Lemon

It's time to fire up the grill and get ready for some serious Mediterranean flavors! Today, we're going to be cooking up a beautiful, juicy Grilled Mediterranean Sea Bass with Olive Tapenade and Lemon, and I promise you, this dish is going to blow your taste buds out of the water (pun intended).

Now, let's gather our ingredients. You'll need:

- 1 whole sea bass, scaled and gutted
- 1 lemon, thinly sliced
- Salt and pepper, to taste
- 4 tablespoons olive oil
- 1/2 cup pitted kalamata olives
- 2 cloves garlic, minced
- 2 tablespoons capers
- 1/2 teaspoon dried thyme
- 2 tablespoons lemon juice

Are you ready to start? Let's go!

The first step is to get our sea bass seasoned and ready to grill. Rub the inside and outside of the fish with salt, pepper, and 2 tablespoons of olive oil. Place the lemon slices inside the fish, and let it sit for 15 minutes.

While our fish is marinating, let's make the tapenade. In a food processor, pulse the olives, garlic, capers, thyme, and remaining 2 tablespoons of olive oil until a rough paste forms.

Preheat the grill to high heat. Place the sea bass on the grill, skin-side down, and let it cook for about 5 minutes on each side, or until the flesh is opaque and the skin is crispy.

In the meantime, place the tapenade in a small saucepan over low heat, and let it heat up for about 3 minutes. Serve the fish on a platter, topped with the warm tapenade and a squeeze of fresh lemon juice.

I have a hilarious anecdote to share with you! One time, I served this dish at a dinner party, and one of my guests took a big bite of the fish, then made a huge scene and started spitting it out! I was mortified, until I realized that they were just really surprised by how delicious it was.

And now, the moment you've all been waiting for... the nutritional information!

Calories: 368   Carbohydrates: 5g   Sodium: 989mg

Fat: 26g   Protein: 32g   Cholesterol: 97mg

Bon appétit!

52. Salmon with Roasted Red Pepper Sauce and Herbed Quinoa

Ladies and gentlemen, are you ready to tantalize your taste buds with a deliciously healthy dinner tonight? Introducing the delectable Pan-Seared Salmon with Roasted Red Pepper Sauce and Herbed Quinoa!

To whip up this lip-smacking feast, you'll need the following ingredients:

- 4 salmon fillets (6 oz each)
- 2 tablespoons olive oil
- Salt and black pepper to taste
- 1 red pepper
- 1/4 cup chicken broth
- 2 cloves garlic
- 1/4 cup Greek yogurt
- 2 tablespoons lemon juice
- 1/4 teaspoon smoked paprika
- 1/4 teaspoon cumin
- 1/4 teaspoon dried oregano
- 1/4 teaspoon dried thyme
- 1 cup quinoa
- 2 cups chicken broth
- 1/4 cup chopped fresh parsley
- 1/4 cup chopped fresh basil

Alright, now that we've got our ingredients, it's time to get to work! Cooking time will take you around 25-30 minutes, with preparation time of 10 minutes. You'll be serving 4 people with this recipe.

To start, let's get our salmon fillets seasoned and seared. Heat up a large skillet over medium-high heat and add the olive oil. Once hot, add the salmon fillets and cook for about 4-5 minutes on each side, or until it's fully cooked. Set it aside.

Next, let's make the roasted red pepper sauce. Roast the red pepper over a flame or under the broiler, until the skin is charred. Then, peel the skin off, remove the seeds and chop it up. In a blender, combine the roasted red pepper, chicken broth, garlic, Greek yogurt, lemon juice, paprika, cumin, oregano, and thyme. Blend until smooth.

While the sauce is blending, let's work on the herbed quinoa. In a saucepan, bring the chicken broth to a boil. Stir in the quinoa, cover and reduce the heat to low. Cook for about 15-20 minutes, or until all the liquid has been absorbed. Stir in the parsley and basil.

Finally, it's time to assemble the dish! Plate the cooked salmon fillets and top with the roasted red pepper sauce. Serve with the herbed quinoa on the side.

Now, here's a fun fact about salmon. Did you know that salmon is actually a type of fish that's capable of swimming upstream? Well, that's probably why it's one of the healthiest fish you can eat!

As for the nutritional values, here's what you can expect per serving:

Calories: 524   Carbohydrates: 47 g   Fiber: 7 g

Fat: 25 g   Protein: 35 g   Sodium: 524 mg

So, go ahead and enjoy this hearty, healthy, and delicious dinner tonight! Your taste buds will thank you for it!

53. Stuffed Clams with Breadcrumbs, Parsley, and Lemon

Get ready to experience a flavor explosion that will have your taste buds begging for more! Today, we're whipping up a dish that's packed with all the right ingredients to tantalize your senses. That's right, we're talking about Stuffed Clams with Breadcrumbs, Parsley, and Lemon. A dish that's fit for royalty, but also easy enough for a weeknight dinner.

Let's start with the most important part, the ingredients! Get ready to jot these down because trust us, you're going to want to remember them. And if you happen to forget, don't worry, we'll remind you of the magical combination.

- 12 large clams
- 1 cup breadcrumbs
- 1/4 cup freshly chopped parsley
- 1/4 cup grated parmesan cheese
- 2 cloves of garlic, minced
- Juice of 1 lemon
- Salt and pepper to taste
- 2 tablespoons olive oil

Get your timer ready because we're about to embark on a culinary adventure. For cooking, we'll need about 15-20 minutes and for preparation, we estimate about 15-20 minutes as well. So in total, you'll need around 30-40 minutes to whip up this delicious dish.

Let's start by preheating the oven to 400°F. Then, shuck the clams and remove the meat from the shells, but keep the shells intact. In a mixing bowl, combine breadcrumbs, parsley, parmesan cheese, garlic, lemon juice, salt, and pepper. Mix until well combined.

Take each clam shell and place a spoonful of the breadcrumb mixture on top of the clam meat. Then, place the shells on a baking sheet and drizzle with olive oil. Bake in the oven for 15-20 minutes, or until the breadcrumbs are golden brown and the clams are cooked through.

One time, a friend of mine tried to make this dish and ended up using breadcrumbs that had gone stale. Let's just say, it was a disaster and the dish turned out inedible. So, the moral of the story is to always check the expiration date on your breadcrumbs before using them. Trust us, your taste buds will thank you.

Per serving, you can expect to find:

Approximately 70 calories	8 grams of carbohydrates	2 grams of fiber
4 grams of fat	4 grams of protein	

So, there you have it, folks! A delicious, nutritious, and easy-to-make dish that's perfect for any occasion. Get ready to impress your friends and family with this showstopper of a dish!

54. Shrimp Skewers with Charred Tomato and Basil Salsa

A recipe so fresh and flavorful, you'll be saying "Shrimp, who needs 'em?" in no time! Get ready for an adventure in your kitchen with the most amazing Shrimp Skewers with Charred Tomato and Basil Salsa. With a tantalizing combination of juicy shrimps, succulent tomatoes and aromatic basil, this recipe is a party in your mouth and a delight for your senses. So, let's start cooking!"

For this delicious recipe, we'll need the following cast of characters:

- 12 large shrimp, peeled and deveined
- 8 cherry tomatoes
- 8 fresh basil leaves
- 1 lemon, juiced
- 2 tablespoons olive oil
- Salt and black pepper to taste
- 4 metal or wooden skewers

We are looking at a total of 20 minutes of prep time and 10 minutes of cooking time. So, in 30 minutes you'll be able to enjoy this delicious dish. Trust me, it's worth the wait!

The first step is to get the grill or grill pan ready. Preheat the grill to medium-high heat or heat up a grill pan on the stove.

While the grill is heating up, let's make the salsa. In a small bowl, combine the cherry tomatoes, basil, lemon juice, olive oil, salt, and pepper. Set it aside.

Next, it's time to skewer the shrimps. If using metal skewers, soak them in water for 10 minutes to prevent burning. Place three shrimps on each skewer and season with salt and pepper.

Grill the skewers for about 3-4 minutes on each side or until the shrimp are opaque and cooked through.

Serve the grilled shrimp skewers with the Charred Tomato and Basil Salsa on the side. And there you have it, a delicious and healthy dish ready to be devoured in no time!"

A funny story about this recipe. One time, I made this dish for my friends and they were so impressed with the flavors that they kept asking me if there was any secret ingredient. I jokingly replied, 'Yeah, love!' They all laughed, but the truth is, a little love does go a long way in cooking.

Now for the important part, the nutritional information. This dish is not only delicious but also healthy. Here's what you can expect per serving:

Total Calories: 172	Cholesterol: 214 mg	Dietary Fiber: 1 g
Total Fat: 11 g	Sodium: 597 mg	Protein: 16 g
Saturated Fat: 2 g	Total Carbohydrates: 5 g	

55. Seared Scallops with Tomato, Caper, and Olive Relish

Introducing the dish that'll make you say "Oh Scallop Yeah!" - Seared Scallops with Tomato, Caper, and Olive Relish! Imagine plump, juicy scallops, seared to perfection and nestled on a bed of tangy and flavorful relish. It's the perfect balance of salty, briny, and acidic flavors that'll have your taste buds singing.

The cast of characters:

- 12 large scallops (fresh is best, but frozen will do in a pinch)
- 1 cup of diced tomatoes
- 2 tablespoons of capers
- 1/4 cup of pitted kalamata olives
- 2 tablespoons of lemon juice
- 1 tablespoon of olive oil
- Salt and pepper to taste

A handful of chopped fresh parsley for garnish

Now, let's get down to business. Cooking time is approximately 20 minutes, prep time is 10 minutes, and this recipe serves 4 lucky people.

To start, let's get the relish ready. In a bowl, combine the diced tomatoes, capers, kalamata olives, lemon juice, olive oil, salt, and pepper. Give it a good mix, taste it, and adjust the seasoning if needed.

Next, let's give those scallops some love. Heat a large pan over medium-high heat and add a splash of oil. When the pan is hot, gently place the scallops in, making sure they're not touching each other. Let them cook undisturbed for 2-3 minutes on each side until they're golden brown and crispy.

Now, it's time to plate up! Spoon a generous helping of the relish onto a plate, place the seared scallops on top, and sprinkle some chopped parsley for that extra pop of green.

A little anecdote to add some flavor to the dish (pun intended). I once had a seafood restaurant cook the scallops too long, and they turned into rubber balls. Don't be that restaurant, cook your scallops just right!

And finally, the nutritional values per serving:

Calories: 216　　　Cholesterol: 49mg　　　Total Carbohydrates: 5.2g

Total Fat: 12.9g　　　Sodium: 953mg　　　Protein: 20.5g

Enjoy your delicious, healthy, and oh-so-flavorful dish!

56. Baked Cod with Tomatoes, Olives, and Feta Cheese

Ready for a recipe that will make your taste buds dance with joy? Well, hold on to your hats and prepare for a flavor explosion because today, we're cooking up a storm with Baked Cod with Tomatoes, Olives, and Feta Cheese!

For this delicious dish, we'll be needing a handful of ingredients that you can find in your local grocery store. To get the ball rolling, let's talk about the cast of characters:

- 4 (6-ounce) cod fillets
- 4 ripe tomatoes, sliced
- 1/2 cup Kalamata olives, pitted and sliced
- 1/2 cup crumbled feta cheese
- 1/4 cup fresh basil leaves
- 4 tablespoons olive oil
- 1 lemon, sliced into rounds
- Salt and pepper to taste

Now that we have our ingredients ready, let's get to cooking! This recipe takes 30 minutes of preparation time and 30 minutes of cooking time. It's perfect for a quick and easy weeknight dinner or a fancy date night at home. And the best part? You'll only need one pan to make this magical meal!

To start, preheat your oven to 425°F (220°C). Line a baking sheet with parchment paper and arrange the cod fillets in a single layer. Top each fillet with sliced tomatoes, Kalamata olives, crumbled feta cheese, and fresh basil leaves. Drizzle with olive oil and season with salt and pepper to taste. Place lemon slices on top of each fillet and around the pan.

Bake the cod in the oven for 20 to 25 minutes, or until the fish is opaque and flaky. Meanwhile, the tomatoes will caramelize and the feta cheese will become golden and melted. The juicy lemon slices will infuse the dish with a tangy, fresh flavor, and the basil will add a sweet, herby aroma.

An anecdote to share: One time, I made this recipe for a dinner party, and all of my guests were blown away by how delicious it was. They couldn't believe that I had made such a fancy and sophisticated dish in just 30 minutes. They were all clamoring for the recipe, and I felt like a kitchen superhero.

Finally, let's talk about the nutritional values of this dish. Here's a rundown of what you'll be getting in each serving:

Calories: 340	Cholesterol: 72mg	Dietary Fiber: 2g
Total Fat: 25g	Sodium: 759mg	Protein: 26g
Saturated Fat: 6g	Total Carbohydrates: 8g	

So there you have it, folks. A delicious and nutritious meal that's perfect for any occasion. Whether you're cooking for yourself or for a crowd, this Baked Cod with Tomatoes, Olives, and Feta Cheese is sure to impress. Get ready to cook up a storm!

57. Grilled Octopus with Potato, Lemon, and Parsley Salad

Hello, foodies! Are you ready for a journey to the Mediterranean? Today we're going to explore the flavors of the sea with a dish that is not only delicious but also quite a spectacle to serve. I'm talking about Grilled Octopus with Potato, Lemon, and Parsley Salad. It's a dish that can be a little intimidating to make, but trust me, with a little guidance, you'll be cooking it like a pro!

So, what do we need for this journey to the sea? Let's take a look at the ingredients:

- 1 octopus, about 1.5-2 pounds, cleaned
- 2 pounds of potatoes
- 1 lemon, sliced
- 2 garlic cloves, minced
- 1/4 cup of extra virgin olive oil
- Salt and pepper, to taste
- 1/2 cup of parsley, chopped
- 2 tablespoons of red wine vinegar
- 4 tablespoons of lemon juice

Grilling octopus can take some time, but the prep work is quite minimal. This dish will take you about 1 hour and 15 minutes to prepare and cook, and about 10 minutes to prep. So, get ready to fire up the grill, and let's get cooking!

Now that we've got our ingredients together, let's start cooking! First, rinse and clean the octopus thoroughly. Then, place it in a large pot of boiling water and let it cook for about 40 minutes, or until it is tender. While the octopus is cooking, peel and chop the potatoes into bite-sized pieces and place them in a pot of boiling water. Cook for about 10-12 minutes, or until they are tender.

In the meantime, let's make the lemon and parsley salad. In a large bowl, mix together the lemon juice, red wine vinegar, extra virgin olive oil, salt, pepper, and parsley. Set aside.

Once the octopus is cooked, let it cool for a few minutes and then slice it into bite-sized pieces. Heat up the grill to medium-high heat and brush the octopus slices with a little olive oil. Grill the octopus slices for about 2-3 minutes on each side, or until they are slightly charred.

To assemble the dish, place the cooked potatoes on a large platter, top with the grilled octopus slices, and drizzle with the lemon and parsley salad. Serve immediately and enjoy!

So, there I was, at a restaurant in Greece, trying grilled octopus for the first time. I was a little intimidated, but I must say, it was love at first bite. The tender octopus, paired with the tangy lemon and parsley salad, was simply divine. And, to think, I almost passed on trying it! From that moment on, I knew I had to learn how to make it myself.

Now, let's take a look at what you'll be indulging in:

Caloric Value: 574 calories	Cholesterol: 63 mg	Dietary Fiber: 6.2 g
Total Fat: 33.8 g	Sodium: 735 mg	Sugars: 2.2 g
Saturated Fat: 5.3 g	Total Carbohydrates: 49.5 g	Protein: 24.9 g

And there you have it, folks! A delicious and healthy Grilled Octopus

58. Squid Ink Risotto with Shrimp, Tomatoes, and Parsley

Ladies and Gentlemen, gather around because I'm about to reveal the secret to a dish that is as rich in flavor as it is in color. A dish that will take you on a culinary journey to the depths of the ocean. A dish that will make you fall in love with the sea. Presenting to you the one and only, the notorious, the oh-so-satisfying: Squid Ink Risotto with Shrimp, Tomatoes, and Parsley!

Okay, let's talk about what we're going to need to whip up this masterpiece. Just like a secret recipe, the ingredients are key to unlocking the full potential of the dish. So listen up, my friends!

- 1 cup Arborio Rice
- 4 cups of chicken or seafood stock
- 2 tablespoons of olive oil
- 1 diced onion
- 3 cloves of minced garlic
- 1/4 cup of white wine
- 2 tablespoons of tomato paste
- 2 tablespoons of squid ink
- 8-10 large shrimps
- 2 diced tomatoes
- 2 tablespoons of chopped parsley
- Salt and pepper to taste
- 1/2 cup of grated Parmesan cheese
- Lemon wedges for garnish

This dish is worth the wait, my friends! The cooking time for this delectable delight is about 30 minutes. But, as the saying goes, "Good things come to those who wait". So, sit back, relax, and let the magic happen in the kitchen! Before we start cooking, we need to prepare all the ingredients. This will take us about 15-20 minutes, so grab your apron and let's get started! This recipe will serve 4 hungry foodies or 2 very, very hungry foodies. Trust me, one serving is never enough!

Let's start by heating the olive oil in a large saucepan over medium heat. Add the diced onion and cook until soft and translucent, about 5 minutes. Next, add the minced garlic and cook for another minute. Now, pour in the white wine and let it cook until it reduces by half.

Now, it's time to add the secret ingredient that gives this dish its unique flavor and color - the squid ink. Stir in the squid ink and the tomato paste, then add the Arborio Rice and stir to coat the grains in the mixture.

Start adding the stock, one ladleful at a time, stirring constantly until each addition is absorbed before adding the next. This will take about 20-25 minutes. Once the rice is cooked and creamy, stir in the diced tomatoes, shrimps, parsley, and grated Parmesan cheese. Season with salt and pepper to taste.

Serve hot with lemon wedges on the side and enjoy the rich, creamy, and delicious flavors of the sea!

Once upon a time, there was a chef who was searching for a dish that would make his customers swoon with every bite. One day, he stumbled upon the idea of adding squid ink to his risotto. And just like that, a new star was born in the culinary world. People would come from far and wide just to taste this dish, and the chef lived happily ever after, knowing that he had created something truly special.

Nutritional values:

Calories: 550

Sodium: 890mg

Protein: 25g

Fat: 20g

Carbohydrates: 57g

Cholesterol: 100mg

Fiber: 2g

59. ~~Air Fryer Beef and Truffle Fries~~

Ladies and gentlemen, gather around, for we are about to embark on a culinary journey through the beautiful and sunny Mediterranean! And what better way to do that than with a delicious and healthy seafood casserole? This dish is perfect for those who are on a Mediterranean diet and looking for a hearty and flavorful meal. Get ready to put on your chef's hat and get your taste buds ready for a wild ride!

Let's start by gathering all the ingredients we'll need for this amazing casserole. And don't worry, it's a simple list, no rocket science involved. Are you ready? Here we go!

- 1 lb of cod, cut into bite-sized pieces
- 1 lb of shrimp, peeled and deveined
- 1 lb of mussels, cleaned and debearded
- 2 large tomatoes, diced
- 1 large onion, chopped
- 4 cloves of garlic, minced
- 1 cup of Kalamata olives, pitted
- 1 cup of chicken broth
- 1/2 cup of white wine
- 1/4 cup of fresh parsley, chopped
- 2 tbsp of olive oil
- Salt and pepper to taste

This seafood casserole is a breeze to make! The preparation time is a mere 20 minutes and the cooking time is only 30 minutes. So, in just 50 minutes, you'll have a delicious and healthy meal that'll make you feel like you're sitting on the beaches of the Mediterranean!

Let's start by preheating the oven to 375°F. In a large skillet, heat the olive oil over medium heat and sauté the onion and garlic until they're soft and fragrant. Add the diced tomatoes and continue cooking for another 5 minutes. Now, let's add the white wine, chicken broth, and parsley to the skillet and bring the mixture to a boil. Reduce the heat to low and let the mixture simmer for 10 minutes.

Next, let's take a large baking dish and layer the cod, shrimp, mussels, and olives in it. Pour the tomato mixture over the seafood and sprinkle some salt and pepper over it. Place the dish in the oven and bake for 30 minutes, or until the seafood is cooked through and the sauce is bubbly.

The first time I made this casserole, I was nervous. I mean, it's seafood, and seafood can be tricky to cook. But I was pleasantly surprised at how easy and delicious it turned out! My friends and family were so impressed that they asked for seconds and even thirds! I even had my picky eater cousin gobble it up without any complaints. It was a huge success, and I couldn't be happier.

Here's a little bonus for all the health nuts out there. This delicious casserole is packed with all sorts of nutrients that'll make you feel great!

Calories: 380

Sodium: 730mg

Protein: 38g

Total Fat: 18g

Total Carbohydrates: 15g

Cholesterol: 170mg

Dietary Fiber: 4g

And there you have it, folks, a delicious and healthy Mediterranean-style seafood casserole that's sure to become a crowd-pleaser. So go ahead, give it a try and let me know how it turns out!

60. Grilled Tuna Steak with Cucumber, Mint, and Lemon Salad

Alright, let's talk about grilling up a juicy, flavorful tuna steak and serving it with a bright and refreshing cucumber, mint, and lemon salad. This dish is a perfect summertime meal that is sure to impress!

Before we get started, let's gather all the ingredients we'll need:

- 4 Tuna steaks (6 oz. each)
- 1 teaspoon of salt
- 1 teaspoon of black pepper
- 2 tablespoons of olive oil
- 1 cucumber, sliced
- 1/2 cup of fresh mint leaves, chopped
- 2 lemons, juiced

Now, let's get down to business. Cooking time is around 10 minutes and preparation time is 15 minutes. This dish serves 4.

To start, let's season the tuna steaks with salt and pepper and then brush them with olive oil. Fire up the grill and place the steaks on the grates. Let them cook for about 5 minutes on each side or until they're a lovely caramelized brown on the outside but still pink in the middle.

While the tuna is cooking, let's make the cucumber, mint, and lemon salad. Simply mix together the sliced cucumber, chopped mint, lemon juice, and a pinch of salt. This simple yet flavorful salad is the perfect accompaniment to the grilled tuna.

When the tuna is ready, remove it from the grill and let it rest for a few minutes to allow the juices to redistribute. While we're waiting, let's set the table and get ready to enjoy this delicious meal!

An anecdote to share while eating this dish is about the time I went on a fishing trip and caught a giant tuna. I was so excited to show off my catch to my friends, but when I tried to cook it, I realized I had no idea what to do with it. So, I googled "how to cook a tuna steak" and this recipe was the first one that popped up. I made it for my friends and it was a huge hit! We all agreed that it was the best tuna we had ever tasted.

And finally, for all you nutrition nuts out there, here's a breakdown of the nutritional values per serving:

Calorie: 312	Cholesterol: 68mg	Dietary Fiber: 1g
Total Fat: 20g	Sodium: 616mg	Protein: 33g
Saturated Fat: 3g	Total Carbohydrates: 5g	

There you have it, folks! A delicious and healthy meal that is sure to impress your guests and leave you feeling satisfied. Enjoy!

Vegetables

61. Ratatouille

Here's a dish that'll transport you straight to the bustling streets of Marseille! A symphony of flavors and colors, this Ratatouille is a delightful Mediterranean classic that's both delicious and healthy. Get ready to whip up a storm in the kitchen and bring a taste of France to your table.

To make this scrumptious dish, you'll need the following ingredients:

- 2 medium eggplants, diced
- 2 large zucchinis, diced
- 2 bell peppers (red and yellow), diced
- 3 large ripe tomatoes, peeled and diced
- 3 garlic cloves, minced
- 1/2 teaspoon dried thyme
- 1/2 teaspoon dried basil
- Salt and pepper, to taste
- 2 tablespoons olive oil

Here's a pro tip before we get started: dice your vegetables into similar-sized pieces so they cook evenly!

Now, it's time to start cooking! The total cooking time for this delicious Ratatouille is about 50 minutes, with a preparation time of about 15 minutes. It yields 4 servings, so you can enjoy a taste of the Mediterranean with your family or friends.

To begin, heat the olive oil in a large pan over medium heat. Add the diced eggplant, zucchini, bell peppers, and garlic and cook, stirring frequently, until the vegetables have softened, about 10 minutes.

Next, add the diced tomatoes, dried thyme, and dried basil to the pan. Season with salt and pepper to taste and continue cooking until the sauce has thickened, about 20 minutes.

Serve this delightful dish with a side of crusty bread or over a bed of fluffy rice for a complete meal.

An old chef once told me that the secret to the perfect Ratatouille is patience. Don't rush the cooking process, let the flavors develop and meld together for a truly delectable experience.

And for all you health nuts out there, here's a little something to show how nutritious this dish is:

Calories: 140	Total Carbohydrates: 16 g	Vitamin C: 70%
Total Fat: 9 g	Dietary Fiber: 5 g	Calcium: 4%
Saturated Fat: 1 g	Protein: 3 g	Iron: 6%
Sodium: 70 mg	Vitamin A: 30%	

62. Roasted Cauliflower Steaks with Chimichurri

Ladies and Gentlemen, are you ready to up your vegetable game? Well, hold on to your hats and get ready to have your taste buds blown away with the most incredible Roasted Cauliflower Steaks with Chimichurri!

Now, let's go shopping! To make this mouth-watering masterpiece, you will need the following ingredients:

- 1 head of cauliflower
- 3 tablespoons of olive oil
- Salt, to taste
- Freshly ground black pepper, to taste

For the Chimichurri:

- 1 cup packed fresh parsley leaves
- 1/2 cup packed fresh cilantro leaves
- 3 cloves garlic
- 1/4 cup red wine vinegar
- 1/4 cup olive oil
- Salt, to taste

Now, let's talk about the cooking time. It will take you about 30 minutes of preparation time and 25 minutes of cooking time to get this magnificent dish ready. And for how many servings? You guessed it, 4-6.

To start, preheat your oven to 400°F (200°C). Cut the cauliflower into 1 1/2-inch thick steaks, keeping the core intact. Reserve any smaller pieces that fall off and cut into bite-sized florets.

Next, in a bowl, whisk together the olive oil, salt, and pepper. Brush the mixture on both sides of the cauliflower steaks and florets, making sure they are well coated. Transfer to a baking sheet and roast in the oven until tender and browned, about 25 minutes.

While the cauliflower is roasting, let's make the Chimichurri. In a food processor, pulse the parsley, cilantro, garlic, red wine vinegar, olive oil, and salt until well combined.

Once the cauliflower is ready, transfer to a serving platter, drizzle with the Chimichurri, and serve.

Now, let me tell you a funny story about Chimichurri. My grandma used to make the most amazing Chimichurri, and one day, she decided to spice it up a little bit by adding a little too much chili. Boy, was that a mistake! The heat was intense, but we all had a good laugh, and I think it was worth it.

Now, let's talk about the nutrition! Here's what you'll get with every serving:

Caloric value: 153 calories	Sodium: 156 mg	Sugar: 2 g
Total fat: 15 g	Total carbohydrates: 5 g	Protein: 3 g
Cholesterol: 0 mg	Dietary fiber: 2 g	

Enjoy your delicious and healthy Roasted Cauliflower Steaks with Chimichurri!

63. Roasted Red Pepper and Feta Stuffed Portobello Mushrooms

Attention, all mushroom lovers! Are you tired of having the same old boring mushrooms as a side dish or appetizer? Well, buckle up, because we've got a game-changer for you! Introducing the Roasted Red Pepper and Feta Stuffed Portobello Mushrooms. This dish is the epitome of comfort food meets elegance and will have everyone begging for seconds.

Hold on to your hats and grab a pen and paper, because you're about to learn how to whip up some magic in your kitchen! Here's what you'll need:

- 4 large Portobello mushrooms, stems removed
- 1 cup of crumbled feta cheese
- 1/2 cup of roasted red pepper, chopped
- 1/4 cup of breadcrumbs
- 2 tablespoons of olive oil
- 2 garlic cloves, minced
- Salt and pepper to taste
- Fresh basil or parsley to garnish

This dish is the perfect combination of quick and easy. The total time required is approximately 30 minutes, with 10 minutes of preparation time and 20 minutes of cooking time.

This recipe serves 4 people, making it the perfect option for a small dinner party or a cozy night in with the family.

Preheat your oven to 400°F.

In a large mixing bowl, combine the crumbled feta cheese, roasted red pepper, breadcrumbs, olive oil, garlic, salt, and pepper.

With a spoon, scoop the mixture into the center of each Portobello mushroom cap.

Place the mushrooms on a baking sheet and bake for 20 minutes, or until the tops are golden brown and the mushrooms are tender.

Garnish with fresh basil or parsley and serve hot!

One time, I made this dish for a dinner party and everyone raved about it. The host even asked me for the recipe and has since made it several times for their own guests. It's a crowd-pleaser that never fails to impress.

Here's a breakdown of the nutritional values per serving:

Calories: 200   Sodium: 600mg   Fiber: 2g

Fat: 17g   Carbohydrates: 10g   Protein: 7g.

Enjoy your delicious and healthy Roasted Red Pepper and Feta Stuffed Portobello Mushrooms!

64. Grilled Asparagus with Lemon and Parmesan

Ladies and gentlemen, gather around, because today, we're gonna cook up a storm! And it's not just any storm, it's a delicious storm that'll leave your taste buds singing and your stomach feeling oh so satisfied. I present to you, Grilled Asparagus with Lemon and Parmesan! This dish is the epitome of spring in a plate and it's as easy as ABC!

Now, let's talk about the magic ingredients that'll make this dish a hit. Are you ready for this? Here's what you'll need:

- 1 lb. of asparagus, trimmed
- 3 tablespoons of olive oil
- 2 teaspoons of lemon zest
- 2 tablespoons of lemon juice
- Salt and pepper to taste
- ¼ cup of grated Parmesan cheese
- 1 teaspoon of garlic powder

The preparation time for this dish is a mere 10 minutes, and the cooking time is only 10 minutes as well. And, the best part? This dish serves 4 people. So, get ready to have a feast and make some memories!

In a mixing bowl, combine the olive oil, lemon zest, lemon juice, salt, pepper, and garlic powder. Whisk everything together to create a marinade.

Take the trimmed asparagus and toss it in the marinade, making sure each stalk is coated well.

Preheat your grill to high heat. When the grill is hot, place the marinated asparagus on the grates and cook for about 8-10 minutes or until tender and charred. Be sure to flip the asparagus every couple of minutes to ensure even cooking.

Once the asparagus is cooked, take it off the grill and place it on a serving platter. Sprinkle the grated Parmesan cheese on top and voila! You're ready to enjoy a plate of Grilled Asparagus with Lemon and Parmesan.

As I was cooking this dish for the first time, I remembered my grandma. She always used to say that asparagus is a very delicate vegetable and it needs to be treated with love. And that's exactly what I did while cooking this dish, I treated the asparagus with love and care, and it turned out to be the best dish I've ever made!

Per serving, this dish has the following nutritional values:

Calories: 120

Sodium: 140mg

Sugar: 3g

Fat: 10g

Carbohydrates: 7g

Protein: 6g

Cholesterol: 5mg

Fiber: 3g

65. Mediterranean Stuffed Bell Peppers

Ah, the Mediterranean Stuffed Bell Peppers! Such a classic dish, with so much flavor and nutrition packed into each and every bite. It's the perfect way to celebrate the warm sun, calm waters, and laid-back lifestyle of the Mediterranean region.

So, what do we need to make these delightful little peppers? Well, buckle up, because we've got a whole bunch of yummy ingredients to pick up at the market! Here's what you'll need:

- 4 large bell peppers (red, yellow, or green)
- 1 lb ground turkey or beef
- 1 cup cooked quinoa or rice
- 1 can of diced tomatoes (14 oz)
- 1/2 cup chopped onion
- 1/2 cup chopped carrots
- 1/2 cup chopped zucchini
- 1/2 cup crumbled feta cheese
- 1 tbsp dried basil
- 1 tsp dried oregano
- 1 tsp dried thyme
- 1 tsp salt
- 1 tsp black pepper
- 1/4 cup chopped fresh parsley
- 1/4 cup chopped fresh mint
- 3 cloves of garlic, minced
- 2 tbsp olive oil

So, let's start cooking! This dish will take about 35 minutes to prepare and cook, and makes 6 servings.

Begin by preheating your oven to 375°F (190°C). Cut the tops off of the bell peppers and remove the seeds and membranes. In a large skillet, heat the olive oil over medium heat and cook the ground meat until browned. Drain any excess fat and return to the heat. Add the onion, carrots, zucchini, basil, oregano, thyme, salt, and pepper. Cook until the vegetables are tender, about 10 minutes. Stir in the quinoa or rice, diced tomatoes, feta cheese, parsley, mint, and garlic.

Now, the fun part! Stuff each pepper with the filling, making sure they're overflowing with deliciousness. Place the peppers in a baking dish, and bake in the oven for 25 minutes, or until the peppers are tender and the filling is hot.

Here's a fun little fact about bell peppers: did you know that they're not actually a vegetable, but a fruit? It's true! And, because of their sweet and juicy taste, they're a great addition to any meal.

And finally, the moment we've all been waiting for - the nutritional information! Each serving of these Mediterranean Stuffed Bell Peppers packs in:

Calories: 360

Sodium: 760mg

Fiber: 4g

Fat: 20g

Carbohydrates: 26g

Protein: 22g

So, go ahead and tuck into these delicious and nutritious stuffed peppers, and feel the sun, sea, and sand of the Mediterranean wrap around you!

66. Pan-Fried Zucchini and Squash with Mint and Feta

Are you tired of the same old vegetable side dishes? Look no further, my friend! Allow me to introduce you to the tasty, fresh, and vibrant world of Pan-Fried Zucchini and Squash with Mint and Feta.

For this dish, you will need the following ingredients:

- 2 medium zucchinis, sliced
- 2 medium yellow squash, sliced
- 2 tablespoons olive oil
- Salt and pepper, to taste
- 2 tablespoons crumbled feta cheese
- 2 tablespoons chopped fresh mint leaves
- 1 lemon, cut into wedges

Let's start by prepping our veggies! Slice your zucchinis and yellow squash into rounds and set aside.

It's time to cook! Heat up a large pan over medium heat, add your olive oil and wait until it's nice and hot. Toss in your sliced zucchinis and squash, making sure each piece is coated in oil. Season with salt and pepper, to taste. Cook for about 5-7 minutes on each side, until they are nicely browned and tender.

While your veggies are cooking, go ahead and crumble your feta cheese and chop up the fresh mint leaves.

Once your veggies are ready, sprinkle the crumbled feta cheese and chopped mint leaves over the top. Squeeze some fresh lemon juice over everything and give it a good toss. Serve hot with a few lemon wedges on the side.

An Anecdote:

A friend of mine once tried to impress a girl he was interested in by cooking her this dish. She was so impressed with his cooking skills that they ended up dating for a year and a half. Who says cooking can't lead to love?

Nutritional Values per serving:

Calories: 129

Cholesterol: 12mg

Dietary Fiber: 2g

Total Fat: 11g

Sodium: 181mg

Sugars: 4g

Saturated Fat: 3g

Total Carbohydrates: 8g

Protein: 4g

So, what are you waiting for? Grab your pan, some veggies, and let's get cooking!

67. Eggplant Parmesan

Are you looking for a classic, comforting and satisfying meal that will make your taste buds dance with joy? Then look no further, my friends! Introducing the all-time favorite, the one and only, the mighty Eggplant Parmesan! This dish is a true testament to the magic of Italian cuisine, combining eggplants, marinara sauce, mozzarella cheese, and parmesan cheese to create a heavenly, melt-in-your-mouth experience. And guess what? It's not just delicious, it's also incredibly easy to make!

Ha-ha, you thought I was going to forget the most important part, didn't you? Of course not! Here's what you'll need to make this amazing dish:

- 2 large eggplants, sliced into rounds
- 1 cup all-purpose flour
- 2 eggs, beaten
- 2 cups breadcrumbs
- 1 cup marinara sauce
- 1 cup shredded mozzarella cheese
- 1/2 cup grated parmesan cheese
- Salt and pepper, to taste

This dish will take about 45 minutes to cook in the oven, but trust me, it's worth every second of the wait!

It will take about 20 minutes to prep the ingredients and get everything ready for the oven.

This recipe will make about 6 servings, so it's perfect for a family dinner or a cozy night in with your significant other.

Alright, let's get started! First, preheat your oven to 400°F (200°C). While the oven is heating up, prepare three shallow bowls. In the first bowl, place the flour and season it with salt and pepper. In the second bowl, place the beaten eggs. And in the third bowl, place the breadcrumbs.

Now it's time to coat the eggplant slices. Dip each slice of eggplant in the flour mixture, then in the beaten eggs, and finally in the breadcrumbs. Place the coated eggplant slices on a baking sheet lined with parchment paper.

Bake the eggplant slices for 20 minutes, or until they're golden brown. Then, remove the baking sheet from the oven and spoon some marinara sauce on top of each slice. Sprinkle the mozzarella cheese and parmesan cheese on top of the sauce.

Return the baking sheet to the oven and bake for another 15 minutes, or until the cheese is melted and bubbly.

I remember my nonna (that's Italian for grandma) making this dish every Sunday for our big family dinner. She would always make enough to feed an army and we would all gather around the table to enjoy a delicious meal together.

Alright, let's talk numbers. One serving of this dish will provide you with:

380 calories

45g of carbohydrates

9g of fiber

17g of fat

20g of protein

There you have it! A delicious, satisfying, and nutritious meal that's sure to become a family favorite. Enjoy!

68. Grilled Artichokes with Lemon and Garlic

Alrighty! Let's get our taste buds ready for some tangy, garlicky and lemony Grilled Artichokes!

So, to make these juicy, savory artichokes, we're gonna need a handful of ingredients. But before that, I have a question for you, have you ever tried to eat an artichoke without any dipping sauce? It's like trying to enjoy a hot summer day without ice cream. It's just not possible!

Here's the list of ingredients:

- 4 large artichokes
- 4 tablespoons of extra-virgin olive oil
- 4 garlic cloves, minced
- 4 tablespoons of lemon juice
- Salt and pepper to taste

Now, let's get to the fun part! Cooking! This recipe will take about 40 minutes of cooking time and around 10 minutes of preparation time. It's going to be a total of 50 minutes of artichoke ecstasy! And trust me, it's totally worth it. It serves 4 people, but you can always double the recipe if you have a big group of artichoke-loving friends.

First things first, we need to clean and prepare the artichokes. Cut off the top of each artichoke, trim the bottom, and cut off the stems so they can stand upright. Then, use a scissors to snip off the sharp tips of each leaf.

Next, we'll be making a marinade with olive oil, lemon juice, minced garlic, salt, and pepper. Mix all the ingredients in a bowl and give it a good stir. Then, using a pastry brush, brush the marinade all over the artichokes, making sure to get in between the leaves as well.

Now, it's time to get grilling! Place the artichokes on the grill and cover the grill. Cook for 20-25 minutes on each side or until the artichokes are tender and slightly charred.

While the artichokes are cooking, let me tell you a funny story. I once heard of a person who tried to eat an artichoke leaf like a chip. They ended up with more hair on their plate than in their head!

And there you have it, the perfectly grilled artichokes with lemon and garlic! Now, let's talk about the nutritional values, shall we?

Each serving contains approximately:

150 calories	2g Protein	6g Fiber
15g Fat	10g Carbohydrates	4g Sugar

And that's a wrap folks! Enjoy these grilled artichokes with your friends and family and make some memories, just like the one I shared with you. Happy grilling!

69. Caramelized Onion, Tomato, and Feta Tart

Greetings! Today, we'll be venturing on a culinary journey to make the most delicious and mouth-watering Caramelized Onion, Tomato, and Feta Tart. This dish is like a ray of sunshine on a cloudy day, it's warm, comforting, and perfect for all those times when you need to brighten up your day!

Let's start by gathering all the ingredients you'll need to make this tart. You will require:

- 1 refrigerated pie crust (9-inch)
- 3 tablespoons olive oil, divided
- 2 medium onions, thinly sliced
- 2 medium tomatoes, sliced
- 1 teaspoon dried thyme
- Salt and freshly ground pepper, to taste
- 1/2 cup crumbled feta cheese

For our ingredients, we have the star of the show - the onions! Then, we have the supporting cast - the tomatoes and feta cheese, who are here to add a pop of flavor and texture to our dish.

Now, let's get down to the nitty-gritty of the recipe. The preparation time for this dish is around 20 minutes and the cooking time is about 45 minutes. The recipe serves 8 people.

To start, we'll preheat the oven to 375°F and line a 9-inch tart pan with the pie crust. In a large skillet, heat 2 tablespoons of the olive oil over medium heat. Add the onions and cook, stirring occasionally, until they are soft and caramelized, about 25 minutes.

Next, we'll add the sliced tomatoes and thyme to the pan and season with salt and pepper. We'll let the mixture cook for another 10 minutes until the tomatoes are soft. Finally, we'll add the remaining 1 tablespoon of olive oil to the pan and remove it from heat.

Now, it's time to layer the caramelized onions and tomatoes on top of the pie crust. Make sure to spread the mixture evenly and sprinkle feta cheese on top. Bake in the oven for 20 minutes or until the crust is golden brown.

Take the tart out of the oven and let it cool for a few minutes. Then, slice it up and serve it warm. The best part about this dish is that it can be served as a main course, a side dish, or even as an appetizer!

Anecdote: Did you know that the ancient Greeks used to serve tarts as an appetizer to their guests? They believed that serving a sweet tart before the meal would stimulate the appetite and make the guests hungrier. Well, this Caramelized Onion, Tomato, and Feta Tart will surely stimulate your taste buds!

And now, for the nutritional values of this delicious dish.

1 slice of the tart contains approximately:	11.7 grams of fat	4.4 grams of protein
	17.3 grams of carbohydrates	1.4 grams of fiber
191 calories		

So, there you have it! A mouth-watering Caramelized Onion, Tomato, and Feta Tart recipe that's sure to brighten up your day! Bon appetit!

70. Roasted Carrot and Chickpea Salad with Tahini Dressing

Ah, the magnificent roasted carrot and chickpea salad with tahini dressing! A dish that'll make you say, "Wow, carrots can taste this good?"

Let's start with the ingredients you'll need to gather to make this delicious salad. Get ready to write this down because it's a doozy:

- 1 lb. Carrots, peeled and chopped into 1-inch pieces
- 1 can Chickpeas, drained and rinsed
- 1 tbsp Olive Oil
- Salt and Pepper, to taste
- 1/4 cup Tahini
- 2 tbsp Lemon Juice
- 1 clove Garlic, minced
- 2 tbsp Water
- 2 tbsp Parsley, chopped

Now that you've got your ingredients in check, let's move on to the cooking and preparation time. This recipe takes around 45 minutes to prepare and cook, so get ready to get your hands dirty in the kitchen.

For serving, this dish serves 4, so it's perfect for a family meal or a gathering with friends.

To make this roasted carrot and chickpea salad, first, preheat your oven to 400°F. In a large bowl, combine the chopped carrots, chickpeas, olive oil, salt, and pepper. Spread the mixture in a single layer on a baking sheet and roast in the oven for 20-25 minutes, or until the carrots are tender and slightly charred.

Meanwhile, in a small bowl, whisk together the tahini, lemon juice, minced garlic, water, and salt. The dressing should have a smooth consistency. If it's too thick, add a little more water, 1 tablespoon at a time.

In a large serving bowl, combine the roasted carrots and chickpeas with the chopped parsley. Pour the tahini dressing over the salad and toss to coat. Serve immediately.

An Anecdote: I once served this dish to my picky eaters, and they gobbled it up in no time. They were so surprised that carrots could taste so delicious and asked for seconds. It's a great way to sneak in some healthy veggies in their diet.

And lastly, the nutritional values for this dish per serving:

Calories: 299	Cholesterol: 0mg	Dietary Fiber: 7g
Total Fat: 19g	Sodium: 249mg	Sugars: 8g
Saturated Fat: 2g	Total Carbohydrates: 27g	Protein: 10g

Side Dishes

71. Roasted Eggplant with Feta and Mint

Ah, roasted eggplant with feta and mint! Now that's a dish that's equal parts delicious and nutritious. It's a flavor explosion in your mouth, a harmonious dance of tangy, salty, and herbaceous notes. And the best part? You'll feel like you're eating something naughty, but it's actually packed with all the good stuff your body needs!

Alright, let's get down to the nitty-gritty. You'll need the following ingredients:

- 2 large eggplants, sliced into 1/2 inch rounds
- 4 tablespoons olive oil
- Salt and pepper to taste
- 1/2 cup crumbled feta cheese
- 2 tablespoons chopped fresh mint
- Lemon wedges for serving

Preheat your oven to 400°F and grease a large baking sheet. In a large bowl, toss the eggplant rounds with the olive oil and a generous pinch of salt and pepper. Spread the eggplant out in a single layer on the prepared baking sheet. Roast for 25-30 minutes, until tender and lightly golden.

Remove the eggplant from the oven and let it cool for a few minutes. Then sprinkle the feta cheese over the eggplant and sprinkle the mint on top. Serve the roasted eggplant with lemon wedges on the side, so that your guests can squeeze a little extra lemon juice over their serving if they like.

Now, let me tell you a little story about the first time I made this dish. I was hosting a dinner party and I wanted to make something special for my guests. I had a few eggplants in the fridge and I decided to try this recipe. I was a little nervous because I had never made it before, but it turned out to be a huge hit! My guests were raving about how delicious it was and they were all surprised when I told them how easy it was to make.

Alright, let's talk nutrition. This dish packs a nutritious punch, with all the good stuff your body needs! Here are the approximate nutritional values per serving:

Calories: 150	Cholesterol: 12mg	Fiber: 4g
Fat: 12g	Sodium: 381mg	Sugar: 4g
Saturated Fat: 3g	Carbohydrates: 8g	Protein: 6g

There you have it! Roasted eggplant with feta and mint is a delicious and nutritious dish that's perfect for any occasion. So go ahead, give it a try and treat your taste buds to a flavor explosion!

72. Grilled Zucchini and Yellow Squash with Herbs

Hello my friends, it's time to put down the steak knives and pick up the grilling tongs because today we're talking about one of summer's most versatile and delicious side dishes, Grilled Zucchini and Yellow Squash with Herbs! These little guys are the perfect addition to any meal, whether it's a BBQ, potluck, or just a regular old Tuesday. And the best part? You won't have to fight for seconds because everyone will be coming back for thirds, fourths, and fifths! So, get ready to have your taste buds tantalized, your tummy satisfied, and your heart warmed with this Grilled Zucchini and Yellow Squash with Herbs recipe.

Let's start by gathering all the ingredients that we'll need to make this beautiful dish. Now, don't be intimidated by the long list of ingredients, I promise it's not as scary as it looks.

- 4 medium zucchinis, sliced lengthwise 1/2 inch thick
- 4 medium yellow squash, sliced lengthwise 1/2 inch thick
- 1/4 cup extra-virgin olive oil
- 3 cloves garlic, minced
- 2 tbsp chopped fresh basil
- 2 tbsp chopped fresh parsley
- 2 tbsp chopped fresh thyme
- 1 tsp salt
- 1 tsp black pepper
- Juice of 1 lemon
- Fresh grated parmesan cheese

It's time to fire up the grill! This dish will take approximately 15-20 minutes to cook, depending on the heat of your grill. So, sit back, relax, and let's get grilling!

This recipe is quick and easy to prepare, taking only about 15 minutes of your time. So, grab your apron and let's get started.

This Grilled Zucchini and Yellow Squash with Herbs recipe will serve 4 people, so it's perfect for a family of four or a small dinner party. And if you're serving a large crowd, just double the recipe and voila!

The first step is to mix the olive oil, garlic, basil, parsley, thyme, salt, pepper, and lemon juice in a large bowl. Then, add the zucchini and yellow squash slices to the mixture, making sure they are well coated.

Next, heat up your grill to medium-high heat. Place the zucchini and yellow squash slices on the grill, being careful not to overcrowd the grill. Cook the slices for 5-7 minutes on each side, or until they are tender and slightly charred.

Finally, remove the slices from the grill and place them on a serving platter. Sprinkle with parmesan cheese and enjoy!

I remember the first time I made this recipe for my family. My sister took one bite and said, "This is the best vegetable dish you've ever made!" I was so happy to hear that, and it just goes to show that even the pickiest eaters can enjoy a healthy and delicious meal.

Nutritional Values:

Calories: 170

Fat: 14g

Saturated Fat: 2g

Cholesterol: 0mg

Sodium: 460mg

Carbohydrates: 10g

Fiber: 2g

Sugar: 4g

Protein: 4g

73. Ratatouille with Tomatoes, Bell Peppers, and Eggplant

Ladies and gentlemen, we are in for a real treat today! Get ready to tantalize your taste buds with the classic dish from the south of France, Ratatouille with Tomatoes, Bell Peppers, and Eggplant! This recipe is not just a feast for the senses, but it's also a playful combination of different textures and flavors.

To make this lip-smacking dish, we need some ingredients that are not just fresh but also have personalities of their own. Let me introduce you to the stars of the show!

- 3 medium-sized eggplants
- 4 large tomatoes
- 2 red bell peppers
- 2 yellow bell peppers
- 2 cloves of garlic, minced
- 2 tablespoons of olive oil
- Salt and pepper, to taste
- Fresh herbs such as basil or thyme, optional

Before you jump in the kitchen, let me tell you, this dish will take some time, but trust me, the end result is worth it! You will spend around 25 minutes in preparation, and 50 minutes to cook the ratatouille to perfection. And if you are lucky enough to have guests, this recipe will serve 4-6 people.

Now, let's get to cooking! Start by preheating your oven to 375°F. Cut the eggplants, tomatoes, and bell peppers into bite-sized pieces and place them on a baking sheet. Drizzle some olive oil over the vegetables and season with salt and pepper. Roast in the oven for 35-45 minutes or until the vegetables are tender and slightly browned.

In the meantime, heat some olive oil in a large pan over medium heat. Add the minced garlic and cook for a minute or until fragrant. Add the roasted vegetables to the pan and stir gently to combine. Add a handful of fresh herbs if desired, and cook for a few more minutes. And voila! Your Ratatouille with Tomatoes, Bell Peppers, and Eggplant is ready to be served!

An Anecdote: This dish is a personal favorite of mine, and I still remember the first time I made it. I was in college and had a date over for dinner, and I wanted to impress her with my cooking skills. I spent hours in the kitchen, chopping, roasting, and sautéing. And when we finally sat down to eat, it was a real culinary adventure. I was proud of my creation, and she was blown away. I knew right then and there, this dish will forever have a special place in my heart.

Nutritional values per serving:

Calories: 199   Carbohydrates: 16g   Fiber: 7g

Fat: 14g   Protein: 5g   Sodium: 267mg

So, what are you waiting for? Gather your ingredients, put on your apron, and let's get cooking! Bon appétit!

74. Stuffed Artichokes with Lemon and Garlic

Have you ever heard of artichokes, the little round green fellows that look like they're wearing a toupee? Well, they're not just pretty to look at, they're also incredibly delicious! And when they're stuffed to the gills with a mixture of lemon, garlic, and breadcrumbs? Heaven. This recipe is a simple one, but it packs a huge punch of flavor. So, let's get started and learn how to make Stuffed Artichokes with Lemon and Garlic.

Now, let's talk about the ingredients, shall we? To make these Stuffed Artichokes, you will need the following:

- 4 large artichokes
- 1 lemon, zested and juiced
- 4 cloves of garlic, minced
- 1/4 cup of breadcrumbs
- 1/4 cup of grated Parmesan cheese
- 1/4 cup of olive oil
- Salt and pepper, to taste
- 2 tablespoons of chopped fresh parsley (optional)

Cooking time for this dish is about 40 minutes, with a preparation time of about 15 minutes. It serves 4 people, which makes it the perfect dish for a small gathering or family dinner.

Let's start by preparing the artichokes. Rinse them under cold water and trim off the stems so they can sit upright. Cut off the top 1/3 of each artichoke and remove the tough outer leaves. With a spoon, scrape out the fuzzy choke in the center. Squeeze some lemon juice on the artichokes to prevent them from browning.

In a small bowl, mix together the breadcrumbs, lemon zest, garlic, Parmesan cheese, olive oil, salt, and pepper. Spoon the mixture into the center of each artichoke, filling it up and making sure it gets into the crevices. Place the artichokes in a large pot with a steamer basket and add 1 inch of water. Cover the pot and bring to a boil. Reduce heat and steam for 25-30 minutes, or until the artichokes are tender.

I remember the first time I made these Stuffed Artichokes, I was so nervous about getting it right. I had never worked with artichokes before and was worried I would mess it up. But, as it turned out, it was a huge success! My guests were impressed with my culinary skills and I felt like a master chef. From that day on, I have been making these Stuffed Artichokes every chance I get.

Here are the nutritional values per serving:

Calories: 250

Cholesterol: 5 mg

Fiber: 7 g

Fat: 18 g

Sodium: 420 mg

Sugar: 5 g

Saturated Fat: 3 g

Carbohydrates: 22 g

Protein: 7 g

75. Grilled Portobello Mushrooms with Balsamic Glaze

Mushrooms, oh the king of the forest, the delicacy of nature! And when it comes to grilling them, it's a whole new level of flavor and texture. Introducing our next culinary delight - Grilled Portobello Mushrooms with Balsamic Glaze, a dish that will make you want to dance with joy.

Here's what you'll need to gather before embarking on this culinary journey.

- 4 Portobello mushrooms
- 3 tablespoons of extra virgin olive oil
- 1 tablespoon of balsamic vinegar
- 2 garlic cloves, minced
- Salt and pepper, to taste

With these simple ingredients in hand, we'll be whipping up a dish that's both healthy and delicious.

So, put on your apron, and let's get started! The cooking time is 10-12 minutes and the preparation time is around 10 minutes. This dish will serve 2-4 people, depending on how hungry you are.

First, clean the mushrooms with a damp cloth to remove any dirt or debris. Next, combine the olive oil, balsamic vinegar, minced garlic, salt and pepper in a bowl. Brush the mixture over the mushrooms and let it marinate for 10 minutes.

Fire up the grill, or heat a grill pan over medium-high heat, and place the mushrooms gill side up. Brush them with the remaining marinade and grill for 10-12 minutes, or until tender.

When the mushrooms are grilled to perfection, remove them from the heat and transfer to a serving platter. Brush with the remaining marinade and serve hot.

Anecdote: Did you know that the Portobello mushroom is actually the mature form of the Crimini mushroom? It's like a teenager growing into an adult, but in the mushroom world.

And finally, the nutritional values per serving of this dish are:

Calories: 179   Fat: 17g   Fiber: 3g

Protein: 5g   Carbohydrates: 9g

So, what are you waiting for? Try this simple yet elegant dish and impress your guests. Bon Appétit!

76. Sweet Potato Fries with Rosemary and Sea Salt

Ladies and Gentlemen, gather around and prepare your taste buds for a wild ride, because we're about to make some Sweet Potato Fries that will knock your socks off! And trust me, you'll be needing your socks to be off when you're ready to dive into this plate of crispy and flavorful fries.

Now, let's talk about the ingredients that we'll need to make this delicious dish. To make the most out of this recipe, you'll want to gather the following:

- 4 medium-sized sweet potatoes, peeled and sliced into thin fry shapes
- 2 tablespoons of olive oil
- 2 teaspoons of dried rosemary
- 1 teaspoon of sea salt

This recipe is incredibly easy to make and won't take much of your time. It will take approximately 15 minutes to prepare and another 25 minutes to cook. And, it'll make about 4 servings, so it's perfect for a small family dinner or a snack for a few friends.

First, you'll want to preheat your oven to 425°F (220°C). Then, line a baking sheet with parchment paper and set aside.

Next, you'll want to combine the sliced sweet potatoes, olive oil, dried rosemary, and sea salt in a large bowl. Make sure to evenly coat the fries in the mixture.

Now, place the coated sweet potato fries on the prepared baking sheet, making sure to arrange them in a single layer.

Pop the baking sheet in the oven and bake for 25 minutes, flipping the fries halfway through the cooking time to ensure even cooking.

One time, I made these Sweet Potato Fries for a BBQ and they were such a hit that I had to make a second batch. People just couldn't get enough of the crispy texture and the blend of rosemary and sea salt. It was such a joy to see everyone enjoying the dish I had made!

Here's a quick rundown of the nutritional values per serving:

Calories: 146	Sodium: 420mg	Sugar: 4g
Fat: 5g	Potassium: 636mg	Protein: 2g
Saturated Fat: 1g	Carbohydrates: 26g	
Cholesterol: 0mg	Fiber: 4g	

77. Mediterranean-style Grilled Asparagus with Lemon and Parmesan

Ladies and Gentlemen, gather around! It's time to whip up a deliciously healthy side dish that'll leave your taste buds doing a tango. Today, we'll be cooking up some Mediterranean-style Grilled Asparagus with a burst of lemon and a sprinkle of parmesan cheese. Buckle up, it's about to get zesty!

Here's what we'll need to make our Mediterranean marvel:

- 1 bunch of asparagus, trimmed
- 2 tablespoons of olive oil
- 1 lemon, juiced
- 2 cloves of garlic, minced
- 1/4 cup of freshly grated parmesan cheese
- Salt and pepper, to taste

Let's put our aprons on and get ready for the main event! Cooking time for this dish is about 10 minutes, with a preparation time of 5 minutes. This dish serves 4 people and is perfect for those who want to enjoy a healthy and flavorful meal.

First, we'll preheat our grill to medium-high heat and place the asparagus on a large piece of aluminum foil. In a small bowl, mix together the olive oil, lemon juice, garlic, salt, and pepper. Pour this mixture over the asparagus, making sure each stalk is coated.

Next, we'll wrap the asparagus in the foil and place it on the grill. We'll let it cook for about 10 minutes, turning occasionally, until the asparagus is tender and slightly charred.

Once it's done, we'll remove it from the grill and sprinkle it with the freshly grated parmesan cheese. We'll give it a final squeeze of lemon juice and serve it immediately.

Anecdote: Did you know that asparagus has been around for more than 2,000 years and was once considered a luxury food fit for royalty? It's a good thing we can now enjoy it at home, on the grill, with a little bit of lemon and parmesan cheese.

And now, for the moment you've been waiting for, the Nutritional values per serving:

Calories: 126   Carbohydrates: 6 g   Protein: 5 g

Fat: 11 g   Fiber: 2 g

There you have it! A quick and easy dish that is both healthy and delicious. Your taste buds will thank you! Enjoy!

78. Roasted Cauliflower with Tahini and Paprika

Well folks, it's time to get in touch with our inner veggie lover with this Roasted Cauliflower with Tahini and Paprika recipe! This dish is not only healthy, but it's also packed with flavor that'll make even the pickiest eaters ask for seconds.

Here's what we'll need to make this masterpiece:

- 1 head of cauliflower
- 3 tablespoons of olive oil
- 1 tablespoon of tahini
- 1 tablespoon of paprika
- Salt and pepper to taste
- 2 tablespoons of lemon juice
- A handful of chopped parsley for garnish

Time to gather the ingredients, and let's get started!

It takes about 30 minutes to prepare, and 30 minutes to cook this dish. Trust me, the wait is well worth it. This dish serves 4-6 people, so you can enjoy it with your friends and family.

Now, let's get down to the nitty-gritty of the cooking process. First, preheat your oven to 425°F (220°C). Next, chop your cauliflower into bite-sized pieces and place them on a baking sheet. Drizzle the olive oil on top, making sure each piece is coated evenly. Then, sprinkle paprika, salt, and pepper to taste on top. Roast the cauliflower in the oven for 30 minutes, or until they're golden and crispy.

While the cauliflower is roasting, mix the tahini, lemon juice, salt, and pepper in a small bowl. Once the cauliflower is ready, take it out of the oven and drizzle the tahini sauce on top. Sprinkle with some chopped parsley, and you're all set!

A fun fact about cauliflower, it's related to the super healthy cruciferous family, which includes broccoli, Brussels sprouts, and cabbage. So, not only does it taste amazing, but it's also packed with vitamins and minerals that are good for you!

Last but not least, let's take a look at the nutritional values of this delicious dish.

Nutritional values per serving:

Calories: 174	Sodium: 226 mg	Fiber: 3 g
Fat: 15 g	Carbohydrates: 8 g	Protein: 4 g

Enjoy your Roasted Cauliflower with Tahini and Paprika dish and don't forget to share it with your friends and family!

79. Israeli Couscous Salad with Chickpeas, Tomatoes, and Herbs

Buckle up your taste buds, folks! It's time to take a culinary trip to the Middle East with our delicious Israeli Couscous Salad. We're going to take a bunch of fresh ingredients, mix them together, and create a flavor explosion in your mouth. This dish is perfect for summer barbecues, potlucks, or even as a light lunch.

Let's start with the ingredients, but before we do, let me just say, this dish is going to make your kitchen smell amazing. The list includes:

- 1 cup Israeli couscous
- 1 can of chickpeas, drained and rinsed
- 1 cup cherry tomatoes, halved
- 1/2 cup diced red onion
- 1/2 cup chopped fresh parsley
- 1/4 cup chopped fresh mint
- 1/4 cup chopped fresh cilantro
- 1 lemon, juiced
- 2 tablespoons extra-virgin olive oil
- Salt and pepper, to taste

Now, let's talk about the cooking time. It takes about 15 minutes to prepare and 15 minutes to cook. The end result? A mouth-watering salad that serves 4 people.

To make this dish, start by boiling the Israeli couscous in salted water until it's tender, then drain and let it cool. In a large bowl, mix together the chickpeas, tomatoes, onion, parsley, mint, cilantro, lemon juice, and olive oil. Season with salt and pepper to taste. Add the cooked Israeli couscous to the bowl and mix everything together.

An interesting anecdote about this dish is that it was originally made in Israel in the 1950s as a substitute for bulgur wheat, which was difficult to obtain at the time. Israeli couscous has since become a staple in Mediterranean cuisine and is loved for its unique texture and versatility.

Now, for the finale, the nutritional values per serving include:

Calories: 280	Sodium: 220mg	Fiber: 6g
Fat: 11g	Carbohydrates: 39g	Protein: 9g

So, get ready to be transported to the Mediterranean with every bite of this delicious Israeli Couscous Salad. Enjoy!

80. Quinoa and Roasted Vegetable Salad with Feta and Lemon Dressing

Get ready for a flavor explosion with this delectable Quinoa and Roasted Vegetable Salad! Perfect for lunch, dinner, or even as a side dish, this dish is a surefire crowd-pleaser. And the best part? You only need a handful of ingredients to whip it up!

So, let's take a look at what we need to get started!

For our salad, we will require:

- 1 cup of uncooked quinoa
- 2 medium sweet potatoes, diced
- 2 medium carrots, diced
- 1 red onion, diced
- 1 red bell pepper, diced
- 1 yellow bell pepper, diced
- 4 cloves of garlic, minced
- 1/4 cup of olive oil
- 1/4 tsp of sea salt
- 1/4 tsp of black pepper
- 1/4 cup of lemon juice
- 1/4 cup of freshly chopped parsley
- 1/4 cup of freshly chopped basil
- 1/4 cup of crumbled feta cheese

Okay, now that we have our ingredients, let's get down to business!

The cooking time for this beauty of a dish is around 35 minutes, with the preparation time taking roughly 10-15 minutes. And when you're all done, you'll have enough servings for 4 people.

So, here's what you'll need to do:

First things first, preheat your oven to 400°F. While that's happening, rinse and drain the quinoa, and then cook it according to the package instructions.

Next, line a large baking sheet with parchment paper and add the sweet potatoes, carrots, onion, bell peppers, garlic, olive oil, salt, and pepper. Toss everything together until everything is coated evenly.

Pop the baking sheet in the oven and let everything roast for 25-30 minutes, or until the vegetables are tender and lightly charred.

While the veggies are roasting, you can prepare the lemon dressing. In a small bowl, whisk together the lemon juice, parsley, basil, and some additional salt and pepper to taste.

Once the veggies are done, let them cool for a few minutes. In a large bowl, add the cooked quinoa, roasted veggies, and feta cheese. Pour the lemon dressing over the top and give everything a good mix.

And there you have it, a delicious Quinoa and Roasted Vegetable Salad that's sure to please!

Now, here's a little anecdote for you. The first time I made this salad, I brought it to a potluck and it was a hit! People were so surprised that something so healthy could taste so good.

And for all you health nuts out there, here's the rundown of the nutritional value per serving:

276 calories

40g carbohydrates

4g fiber

12g protein

11g fat

11g sugar

Appetizers

81. Stuffed Grape Leaves (Dolmades)

Ladies and Gentlemen, hold on to your hats, because we're about to take a culinary journey to the Mediterranean with these stuffed grape leaves! You might know them as Dolmades, and let me tell you, they are a delight to the taste buds. But before we dive into the recipe, let's gather the ingredients first.

Ingredients:

- 1 cup of long grain white rice
- 1 medium yellow onion, finely chopped
- 1/4 cup of fresh parsley, chopped
- 1/4 cup of fresh mint, chopped
- 1/4 cup of fresh dill, chopped
- 2 tablespoons of olive oil
- 2 tablespoons of lemon juice
- 1 teaspoon of sugar
- 1 teaspoon of salt
- 1/4 teaspoon of black pepper
- 36-40 grape leaves, rinsed and drained
- 1 cup of water
- 1/2 cup of lemon juice
- 1/4 cup of olive oil

For the grape leaves, you can either buy them fresh or canned. If you opt for the latter, make sure to rinse them thoroughly and let them soak in cold water for at least 30 minutes to soften.

Now, let's talk about the cooking and preparation time. To bring these delicious stuffed grape leaves to life, it'll take you about 45 minutes to prepare and another 45 minutes to cook. And voila! You'll have a scrumptious dish that can feed 6-8 people.

To start, let's mix the rice, onion, parsley, mint, dill, 2 tablespoons of olive oil, 2 tablespoons of lemon juice, sugar, salt, and pepper in a large bowl. Next, take a grape leaf, place a heaping teaspoon of the mixture on the stem end, fold the sides over the filling, and roll up tightly. Repeat with the remaining ingredients.

In a large saucepan, arrange the stuffed grape leaves seam side down. Pour 1 cup of water, 1/2 cup of lemon juice, and 1/4 cup of olive oil over the stuffed leaves. Place a heat-proof plate on top to keep the leaves in place and prevent them from unraveling. Bring the mixture to a boil, then reduce heat and let it simmer for about 45 minutes, or until the liquid is absorbed and the rice is fully cooked.

I remember my grandma making these Dolmades for special occasions, and the whole house would smell like a Mediterranean paradise. She would always tell us that the secret to a good Dolmades is in the stuffing, so make sure to use fresh herbs and enough spices to bring out the flavors.

Now, for the moment of truth, let's check the nutritional values.

Per serving (based on 8 servings):

Calories: 176

Sodium: 438mg

Protein: 3g

Fat: 12g

Carbohydrates: 16g

Fiber: 2g

And there you have it! A healthy, delicious, and visually stunning dish that will transport your taste buds to a sun-kissed, scenic village on the Aegean coast. Get your forks ready, and let's dig in!

82. Grilled Eggplant Rolls with Feta and Mint

Eggplants, cheese, and mint, oh my! Get ready for a Mediterranean-style flavor explosion with this delicious dish. Grilled eggplant rolls with feta and mint are a perfect side dish or appetizer for any summer gathering. Think of it as a lighter version of lasagna but with a fresh twist, perfect for a summertime feast!

Before we dive into the ingredients, let me tell you a funny story. So, I once made these eggplant rolls for a potluck, and my friends kept asking me if they were vegan because they were so light and fluffy. I had to break the news to them that it was feta cheese in there. They were still in disbelief, but they still loved it!

Ingredients:

- 2 large eggplants, sliced lengthwise into thin rounds
- Salt and pepper
- 1/4 cup olive oil
- 1/2 cup crumbled feta cheese
- 2 tablespoons fresh mint, chopped
- 2 tablespoons lemon juice
- 1 clove of garlic, minced
- 1/2 teaspoon paprika

Preparation and cooking time:

20 minutes prep time, 20 minutes cooking time

Servings: 6

Here we go, it's time to get our grilling on! Start by slicing the eggplants lengthwise into thin rounds, and then sprinkle with salt and pepper. Brush each slice with olive oil and grill until tender, around 4 minutes on each side. While the eggplant is grilling, mix together the crumbled feta cheese, mint, lemon juice, minced garlic, and paprika in a bowl.

As you lay the grilled eggplant slices on a plate, place a spoonful of the feta mixture at one end of each slice and roll it up. Voila! You now have yourself a tray of gorgeous and delicious grilled eggplant rolls.

Now, here's a little anecdote for you. I once made these rolls for a dinner party, and they disappeared within minutes! I had to make a second batch just to keep up with the demand. They're that good!

And for those who are curious about the nutritional values, here's what you get per serving:

Calories: 156   Protein: 4g   Fiber: 3g

Fat: 14g   Carbohydrates: 8g

So go ahead, fire up the grill, and get ready for a flavor explosion! Your taste buds will thank you.

83. Roasted Red Pepper and Feta Dip

Ladies and Gentlemen, gather 'round because I have a delectable recipe to share with you all today! Get ready for a flavor explosion, as we dive into the world of Roasted Red Pepper and Feta Dip!

Before we get started, let me give you a heads up, this dip is not for the faint-hearted. It's packed with bold and tangy flavors, that'll have you reaching for more, with every dip. So, get your crackers, carrots, or chips ready, and let's dive in!

Here's what you'll need to make this lip-smacking dip:

- 2 large red bell peppers, roasted and peeled
- 1/2 cup crumbled feta cheese
- 1/2 cup plain Greek yogurt
- 1/4 cup chopped fresh parsley
- 2 cloves garlic, minced
- 2 tablespoons freshly squeezed lemon juice
- Salt and pepper, to taste
- 1/4 cup extra-virgin olive oil

Preparation time: 15 minutes, Cooking time: 20 minutes, Servings: 4-6

So, to get started, let's first roast the red bell peppers. You can do this by placing them on a baking sheet and broiling them in the oven, until the skin is charred and bubbly. Once that's done, peel off the skin and chop the peppers into small pieces.

Next up, take a large mixing bowl and add in the roasted red peppers, crumbled feta cheese, Greek yogurt, chopped parsley, minced garlic, lemon juice, salt, pepper, and olive oil. Mix everything together until well combined.

Now, for the fun part, let's bake this dip to perfection! Preheat your oven to 375°F, and transfer the dip into an oven-safe dish. Bake for 20 minutes, or until the dip is hot and bubbly.

An anecdote to share with you all, I remember the first time I made this dip. I was hosting a small get-together, and as soon as I put this dip out on the table, it was devoured within minutes. My guests couldn't get enough of it and were asking for the recipe. And that's when I knew, this Roasted Red Pepper and Feta Dip was a crowd-pleaser.

Now, for the nutritional information:

Calories: 186	Cholesterol: 20mg	Fiber: 2g
Fat: 18g	Sodium: 455mg	Sugar: 3g
Saturated Fat: 5g	Carbohydrates: 7g	Protein: 6g

And there you have it, a simple, yet delicious recipe for Roasted Red Pepper and Feta Dip. Serve it as an appetizer, snack, or even as a spread for your sandwiches. Trust me, once you make this, you'll never look back!

84. Marinated Olives and Feta

Get your taste buds ready for a flavor explosion!" That's what I like to say when I'm about to make this delicious Marinated Olives and Feta dish. It's simple, flavorful and a perfect appetizer to get your dinner party started!

Let's take a look at the ingredients we'll need:

- 1 cup of mixed olives, pitted
- 1/4 cup crumbled feta cheese
- 2 cloves of garlic, minced
- 2 tbsp of lemon juice
- 2 tbsp of olive oil
- 1 tsp of dried oregano
- Salt and black pepper to taste

Now that we've got our ingredients ready, let's get to it!

This dish takes no time at all to prepare. Just 10 minutes to be exact. And as far as cooking time goes, well, there's no need to even turn on the stove, it's that easy!

So, what are we waiting for? Let's get started!

First, mix the olives, feta cheese, minced garlic, lemon juice, olive oil, oregano, salt, and pepper in a large bowl. Make sure everything is well combined.

Next, transfer the mixture to an airtight container and refrigerate for at least 2 hours, or overnight for best results.

Serve chilled or at room temperature with some crusty bread or crackers. Perfect for a party, gathering, or just a lazy night in with friends.

Here's a fun fact, did you know that the ancient Greeks used to make a similar dish as an offering to their gods? It just goes to show you how timeless this dish truly is!

As far as nutritional values go, a serving of this Marinated Olives and Feta dish provides:

Calories: 107   Carbohydrates: 2g

Fat: 11g   Protein: 2g

So, there you have it, a delicious and easy-to-make appetizer that's not only packed with flavor but also has some healthy benefits! Serve it up and watch it disappears!

85. Fried Zucchini with Yogurt Dip

Oh boy! Are you ready for a taste explosion? This delicious recipe is perfect for those hot summer nights, when you just want something fresh, crispy and satisfying. I'm talking about Fried Zucchini with Yogurt Dip, a light and tangy dish that will leave you feeling like you just won the culinary lottery.

Hold on to your hats, because the ingredients list is short, sweet, and oh so delicious!

- 4 medium-sized zucchinis, sliced into rounds
- 1 cup of all-purpose flour
- 2 teaspoons of paprika
- Salt and pepper, to taste
- 2 large eggs, lightly beaten
- 2 cups of panko breadcrumbs
- Oil, for frying
- 1 cup of Greek yogurt
- 1 clove of garlic, minced
- 1 tablespoon of lemon juice
- Fresh mint leaves, chopped

You'll only need about 20 minutes to fry up the zucchini to crispy, golden perfection.

Before you start frying, you'll want to spend about 10 minutes getting everything prepped and ready to go.

This recipe will make 4 servings, which is perfect for a light summer dinner or as an appetizer to share with friends.

Let's get started! In a shallow bowl, whisk together the flour, paprika, salt and pepper. In another shallow bowl, beat the eggs and in a third shallow bowl, mix the panko breadcrumbs.

Dip each zucchini slice first in the flour mixture, then in the eggs, and finally in the panko breadcrumbs. Repeat the process until all the zucchini slices are coated.

Heat the oil in a large frying pan over medium heat. Once hot, add the zucchini slices in a single layer, without overcrowding the pan. Fry until the zucchini is golden brown on both sides, about 2-3 minutes per side.

While the zucchini is frying, mix the yogurt, garlic, lemon juice, and mint leaves in a small bowl. Serve the fried zucchini with the yogurt dip on the side.

This dish is a staple in Mediterranean cuisine and is a classic summertime treat. When I was a kid, my family and I would spend our summer vacations in Greece and we would always stop by this little street food stand and get a plate of Fried Zucchini with Yogurt Dip. It always brought back such happy memories!

This dish is not only delicious, but it's also nutritious! Here's what you can expect in each serving:

Calories: 397   Sodium: 578mg   Protein: 16g

Fat: 19g   Carbohydrates: 43g   Fiber: 6g

86. Spinach and Feta Puffs (Spanakopita)

Once upon a time in Greece, there was a dish so delicious, so savory, so mouth-watering that it quickly became a staple in the Greek cuisine. That dish, my friends, is none other than Spinach and Feta Puffs, or as the Greeks call it, Spanakopita!

So, what do you need to create this delightful dish? Well, gather around, because I've got a list of ingredients that will make your taste buds dance with joy:

- 2 tablespoons olive oil
- 1 large onion, chopped
- 2 garlic cloves, minced
- 2 bunches of fresh spinach, washed, stems removed, and chopped
- 1 cup crumbled feta cheese
- 1/2 cup ricotta cheese
- 1/4 cup grated Parmesan cheese
- 1/4 cup chopped fresh mint
- Salt and freshly ground black pepper
- 1 package phyllo dough, thawed
- 1/2 cup unsalted butter, melted

Now that we have our ingredients together, let's talk about the cooking time and preparation. To make these Spinach and Feta Puffs, you'll need to set aside about an hour of your time. 30 minutes of preparation time and 30 minutes of cooking time. And the best part? You'll get to enjoy 12 servings of these amazing little puffs.

First, heat the olive oil in a large saucepan over medium heat. Add the onion and garlic and cook until softened, about 5 minutes. Stir in the spinach and cook until wilted, about 5 minutes. Transfer the mixture to a large bowl and let it cool. Once cooled, add the feta, ricotta, Parmesan, and mint and mix well. Season with salt and pepper to taste.

Preheat your oven to 375°F (190°C). On a lightly floured surface, unfold the phyllo dough and cover with a damp cloth. Take one sheet of phyllo and brush it with melted butter. Top with another sheet of phyllo and brush it with melted butter. Repeat with the remaining phyllo, ending with a buttered sheet. Cut the phyllo stack in half lengthwise and then into 12 equal squares.

Place a heaping tablespoon of the spinach mixture in the center of each square. Fold the corners of the square up and around the filling to form a triangle. Place the puffs on a baking sheet lined with parchment paper. Brush the tops of the puffs with melted butter. Bake until golden brown, about 20 minutes. Serve the puffs warm with a bowl of Greek yogurt on the side.

Anecdote: Did you know that Spanakopita is a popular street food in Greece? It's often sold in bakeries and street food stalls, and it's a staple in many households. It's the perfect snack to grab on the go or to serve as an appetizer at a dinner party. Your guests will be impressed with your culinary skills and will be begging for more.

Nutritional values per serving:

Calories: 170

Fat: 14 g

Saturated fat: 7 g

Cholesterol: 30 mg

Sodium: 470 mg

Carbohydrates: 9 g

Fiber: 2 g

Sugar: 1 g

Protein: 6 g

87. Fried Artichokes with Lemon Aioli

Are you ready for an adventure in the kitchen? Well, buckle up because we are going on a culinary journey to create some deliciously crispy and tangy Fried Artichokes with Lemon Aioli. This dish is like taking a trip to the Mediterranean without ever leaving your kitchen!

For the ingredients, let's see what we need:

- 4 large artichokes
- 1 cup of all-purpose flour
- 1 teaspoon of garlic powder
- Salt and pepper to taste
- 2 cups of vegetable oil for frying
- And for the aioli:
- 1 cup of mayonnaise
- 2 cloves of garlic, minced
- 2 tablespoons of lemon juice
- Salt and pepper to taste

Alright, so now that we have the ingredients, let's get to the cooking part. To make the aioli, simply mix all of the ingredients together in a bowl and let it sit in the fridge for at least an hour.

As for the artichokes, we want to prep them by cutting off the top and bottom, then removing the tough outer leaves. Cut the artichokes in half and remove the prickly center. Slice the artichokes into thin rounds and mix them with the flour, garlic powder, salt, and pepper.

It's time to heat up the oil in a large pan and start frying the artichokes until they are golden brown. This should take about 2-3 minutes on each side. Once they are crispy and done, let them drain on a paper towel-lined plate.

Now it's time to serve these bad boys up with a dollop of the lemon aioli and a squeeze of lemon juice. Perfect for a fun and summery snack or even as a side dish for your next dinner party.

An anecdote: I once made this dish for a potluck and let's just say, it was gone before I even had a chance to try it! My friends couldn't get enough of the crispy and tangy artichokes paired with the creamy and zesty aioli.

And lastly, let's take a look at the nutritional values per serving (assuming 8 servings):

Calories: 366	Cholesterol: 11mg	Dietary Fiber: 7g
Total Fat: 39g	Sodium: 443mg	Sugar: 4g
Saturated Fat: 5g	Total Carbohydrates: 21g	Protein: 5g

So there you have it, a delicious and unforgettable dish that is sure to please your taste buds and impress your friends and family. Enjoy!

88. Baked Feta with Honey and Thyme

Baked Feta with Honey and Thyme" - A Recipe to Woo Your Taste Buds!

Ladies and gentlemen, are you ready to treat your taste buds to an experience they will never forget? Well, buckle up, because we're going to make the most delectable, mouth-watering dish you'll ever lay your eyes (and tastebuds) on. We're talking about none other than "Baked Feta with Honey and Thyme". This dish is like a warm hug from your grandma on a cold day - comforting, flavorful and simply irresistible!

Here's what you'll need:

- 1 block of feta cheese, about 8 ounces
- 2 tablespoons of honey
- 1 tablespoon of thyme leaves
- 1 tablespoon of extra-virgin olive oil
- Salt and pepper to taste
- Fresh thyme for garnish (optional)

Preheat the oven to 400°F and grab a baking dish. Now, let's move on to the next step, which is the preparation time. This dish is so simple to make that you won't even break a sweat. It takes only 5 minutes to prepare and 20 minutes to cook. And before you know it, you'll be savoring every bite of this delicious dish!

Now, let's get to the part where the magic happens. In a small bowl, whisk together the honey, thyme leaves, olive oil, salt and pepper. Place the block of feta cheese in the center of the baking dish and pour the mixture over it. Pop it in the oven and let it bake for 20 minutes, or until the cheese is soft and gooey.

Here's a fun fact, did you know that the ancient Greeks used to serve feta cheese as a dessert? It was sweetened with honey and served as a treat after a meal. How cool is that?!

Finally, it's time to serve! Take the feta cheese out of the oven, let it cool for a couple of minutes, and then serve it with crackers or toasted bread. If you're feeling fancy, you can sprinkle some extra thyme leaves on top for garnish.

Now, let's talk about the nutritional values. This dish is a great source of protein, healthy fats, and is low in carbohydrates. Here's a breakdown of the nutritional values per serving (based on 8 ounces of feta cheese):

Calories: 300	Carbohydrates: 13g	Protein: 12g
Fat: 25g	Fiber: 0g	
Sodium: 1320mg	Sugar: 13g	

So, there you have it, folks! "Baked Feta with Honey and Thyme" - a dish that's not only delicious but also nutritious. Who says you can't have your cheese and eat it too? Happy cooking!

89. Roasted Eggplant and Tomato Bruschetta

Let's talk about the perfect appetizer for your next dinner party, a dish that will leave your guests impressed and their taste buds tantalized. I'm talking about the Roasted Eggplant and Tomato Bruschetta, a simple yet flavorful Mediterranean dish that's both healthy and delicious!

Now, before we get into the nitty-gritty of the recipe, let's talk about the ingredients.

For this recipe, you'll need:

- 1 large eggplant, sliced into rounds
- 2 large tomatoes, chopped
- 4 cloves of garlic, minced
- 2 tablespoons olive oil
- 1 teaspoon balsamic vinegar
- Salt and pepper, to taste
- 4 slices of crusty bread, toasted
- Fresh basil leaves, for garnish
- Grated Parmesan cheese, for garnish

This dish is incredibly easy to prepare and will only take you around 30 minutes to cook. So, pour yourself a glass of wine, turn on some tunes, and let's get started!

The preparation time for this dish is also quick, clocking in at around 15 minutes. So, no need to spend hours in the kitchen to impress your guests!

This recipe yields 4 servings, so it's perfect for a small dinner party or even a casual night in with your loved ones.

To start, preheat your oven to 400°F and line a baking sheet with parchment paper.

Next, place the sliced eggplant on the prepared baking sheet, drizzle with olive oil, and season with salt and pepper. Roast for 25-30 minutes, or until the eggplant is tender and slightly golden.

While the eggplant is roasting, mix together the chopped tomatoes, minced garlic, balsamic vinegar, and remaining olive oil. Season with salt and pepper, to taste.

Once the eggplant is done, remove it from the oven and let it cool slightly.

To assemble the bruschetta, top each slice of toasted bread with a few eggplant rounds, a spoonful of the tomato mixture, and a sprinkle of grated Parmesan cheese.

Garnish with fresh basil leaves and serve immediately.

I remember the first time I made this dish for my family. They were all skeptical about the eggplant, but once they took a bite, their eyes lit up, and they couldn't stop raving about it. I guess you could say that this Roasted Eggplant and Tomato Bruschetta converted my whole family into eggplant fans!

Per serving, this dish contains:

Calories: 216

Sodium: 443mg

Fiber: 7g

Fat: 12g

Carbohydrates: 23g

Protein: 7g

So, there you have it, a delicious and healthy Mediterranean dish that's sure to impress your guests. Give it a try and let me know what you think in the comments below, or better yet, write a review on Amazon!

90. Marinated Mushrooms with Herbs and Garlic

Are you ready to bring the earthy, umami-rich flavors of mushrooms to your kitchen with a bang? Well, buckle up, buttercup, because this Marinated Mushrooms with Herbs and Garlic recipe is going to take you on a delicious journey you'll never forget!

For this recipe, you'll need the following ingredients:

- 1 lb (450 g) of mixed mushrooms, sliced
- 1/2 cup (120 ml) of olive oil
- 3 cloves of garlic, minced
- 2 tbsp (30 ml) of white wine vinegar
- 1 tbsp (15 g) of Dijon mustard
- 2 tsp (5 g) of dried thyme
- 2 tsp (5 g) of dried basil
- Salt and pepper, to taste

So, let's get our hands dirty and make some magic happen in the kitchen!

Cooking time for this recipe is a mere 20 minutes, but the preparation time might take a little longer because you'll have to chop up all those gorgeous mushrooms. But trust me, it's worth it! This recipe makes about 4 servings, so you can enjoy these delicious bites with your friends and family.

Now, let's get to the fun part. To start, you'll want to combine all the ingredients, except the mushrooms, in a large bowl and whisk together to form the marinade. Add the sliced mushrooms to the bowl, making sure they are coated evenly. Let the mushrooms sit and marinate in the fridge for at least an hour, or even better, overnight.

When you're ready to cook, simply place the mushrooms on a baking sheet and bake in a preheated oven at 400°F (200°C) for 20 minutes. That's it! The aroma of the herbs and garlic will fill your kitchen and your taste buds will be tantalized with every bite.

I once served these mushrooms as an appetizer at a dinner party, and one of my guests was so enamored with them that they ate the entire serving by themselves. I think that's the highest compliment a cook can receive, don't you?

And now, let's talk about the nutritional information. Each serving of Marinated Mushrooms with Herbs and Garlic contains:

Calories: 199	Cholesterol: 0 mg	Dietary Fiber: 2 g
Total Fat: 18 g	Sodium: 251 mg	Protein: 4 g
Saturated Fat: 2 g	Total Carbohydrates: 6 g	Sugars: 2 g

So, go ahead and indulge in this delicious recipe without any guilt! Your taste buds will thank you.

91. Greek Yogurt with Honey and Walnuts

Aha! I have a delicious and easy recipe for you, the one that will make you feel like a Greek god/goddess in just a matter of minutes. Presenting to you the "Greek Yogurt with Honey and Walnuts" - A divine creation that will tantalize your taste buds, leaving you asking for more.

Hold on to your horses folks! Before we dive into the recipe, let's gather some ingredients for the dish. It's a short list, so don't worry about getting lost in the supermarket.

- 2 cups of Greek yogurt
- 3 tablespoons of honey
- 1 cup of walnuts
- 2 tablespoons of raisins (optional)
- A pinch of cinnamon

This recipe is incredibly quick and effortless, the perfect dessert for when you want something sweet and indulgent. Cooking time will only take you 5 minutes, and the preparation time is 10 minutes. And the best part? You can feed up to 4 people with this divine creation.

To start, take a big bowl and add 2 cups of Greek yogurt in it. Stir in 3 tablespoons of honey and mix it until well combined. Now, take 1 cup of walnuts and chop them into small pieces, add them to the yogurt mixture. If you're feeling adventurous, you can also add 2 tablespoons of raisins for an extra crunch. Sprinkle a pinch of cinnamon and mix everything together.

Now, take four bowls and evenly distribute the yogurt mixture among them. Top each bowl with some extra chopped walnuts and drizzle some honey over the top. And there you have it, folks! A delicious and healthy dessert that's ready in no time.

I remember one time, I made this recipe for my friends, and they were in awe of its simplicity and taste. They kept asking me for the recipe, and I had to share it with them. Since then, they've been making it all the time, and I'm so glad that I could bring a smile to their faces with this dish.

To make sure that you're aware of what you're putting in your body, here's a list of the nutritional values of this recipe:

Calories: 310	Cholesterol: 5 mg	Fiber: 2 g
Fat: 23 g	Sodium: 95 mg	Sugar: 18 g
Saturated Fat: 4 g	Carbohydrates: 20 g	Protein: 12 g

Now, you can enjoy this delicious dessert without any guilt. I hope you enjoy it as much as I do!

92. Baklava

Introducing the sweet and sticky delight that is Baklava! This delectable dessert has been a staple in Middle Eastern cuisine for centuries and for good reason. The flaky layers of phyllo dough, the nutty filling, and the sticky syrup make for a truly mouth-watering experience.

To make this delicious treat, you'll need the following ingredients:

- 1 cup of unsalted butter, melted
- 1 pound of phyllo dough
- 2 cups of chopped walnuts
- 1 cup of sugar
- 1 tsp. of cinnamon
- 1/2 cup of honey
- 1/2 cup of water
- 1 lemon, juiced

Now, let's get down to business! To start, preheat your oven to 350°F and grease a 9x13 inch baking dish. Next, let's make the filling by mixing together the chopped walnuts, sugar, and cinnamon.

As for preparation time, allow yourself about 30 minutes to get everything ready and in the oven. Cooking time will take a little over an hour, but it's well worth the wait. This recipe makes enough for 24 servings of sweet, sticky, and satisfying Baklava.

Now, let's assemble this delicious dessert! First, place a layer of phyllo dough in the bottom of the greased baking dish. Then, brush with melted butter. Repeat with 9 more layers of phyllo dough, brushing each layer with melted butter.

Next, sprinkle half of the nut mixture on top of the phyllo layers. Repeat the phyllo and nut layers until all the ingredients are used. End with a top layer of phyllo.

Using a sharp knife, make diagonal cuts in the top layer of phyllo to form diamond shapes. Bake for 60-70 minutes, or until the top is golden brown.

While the Baklava is baking, let's make the syrup! In a saucepan, combine the honey, water, and lemon juice. Heat over medium heat until the sugar is dissolved. Once the Baklava is finished baking, remove it from the oven and immediately pour the syrup over the top. Let it cool completely before serving.

An old Baklava making legend states that the more layers of phyllo in your Baklava, the more prosperous and successful you will be in the coming year. So, go ahead and add a few extra layers for good measure!

And now for the nutrition facts:

Calories: 295	Sodium: 31mg	Protein: 4g
Fat: 18g	Carbohydrates: 33g	Cholesterol: 31mg

93. Rosewater and Pistachio Panna Cotta

Ladies and Gentlemen, let me tell you a story about a dessert that is not only delightful but also has a touch of royalty in every bite. Introducing the Rosewater and Pistachio Panna Cotta! A dessert that has been cherished by Kings and Queens of the past and is now gracing the tables of commoners like us. Get ready to be transported to a world of decadence and luxury with this beautiful creation.

Now, let's talk about the ingredients that are needed to make this delicious dessert. To be honest, you don't need a long list of exotic ingredients to make this, just a few basic ingredients and some love!

- 2 cups of heavy cream
- 1 cup of whole milk
- 1/2 cup of sugar
- 2 teaspoons of unflavored gelatin
- 2 tablespoons of cold water
- 1 teaspoon of rose water
- 1/2 teaspoon of vanilla extract
- 1/2 cup of chopped pistachios

This dessert is not only a treat for the taste buds but also for the eyes. And the best part? It's not that hard to make! It will take you only 20 minutes to prep and 2 hours to set. So, sit back, relax and let's get started!

Start by softening the gelatin in cold water and set it aside. In a medium saucepan, mix together cream, milk, sugar, and vanilla extract. Place the saucepan over medium heat and cook until the sugar has dissolved. Stir in the rose water and the softened gelatin. Once the mixture is smooth, pour it into 4 ramekins or cups. Sprinkle chopped pistachios on top and refrigerate for 2 hours or until set.

One of the stories about Panna Cotta is that it was created by a 16th-century chef who was trying to impress a king with a new dessert. But instead of using traditional ingredients like honey and nuts, he used heavy cream, sugar, and vanilla. The King was so impressed with the dessert that he declared it the official dessert of the Kingdom. And that, my friends, is how Panna Cotta became a classic dessert!

And finally, let's talk about the nutritional values of this beautiful dessert.

Energy: 300kcal	Cholesterol: 85mg	Fiber: 1g
Fat: 23g	Sodium: 55mg	Sugar: 16g
Saturated Fat: 14g	Carbohydrates: 19g	Protein: 6g

And that, folks, is the recipe for the most delicate and delicious dessert you'll ever have, the Rosewater and Pistachio Panna Cotta. It's a treat for both the eyes and the taste buds. Enjoy!

94. Orange and Almond Olive Oil Cake

"Sugar, spice, and everything nice!" - have you heard of this phrase? Well, I like to think of it as the ingredients to a perfectly baked Orange and Almond Olive Oil Cake! This sweet, citrusy, and nutty delight is the perfect way to brighten up your day and make your taste buds dance with joy. Let me tell you, this cake is like a warm hug on a cold winter day and a ray of sunshine on a hot summer day, all in one!

Here's what we'll need to whip up this divine treat:

- 3 large eggs, room temperature
- 1 cup granulated sugar
- 1/2 cup freshly squeezed orange juice
- 1/2 cup olive oil
- 1/2 cup almond flour
- 1/2 teaspoon baking powder
- 1/2 teaspoon baking soda
- 1/2 teaspoon salt
- 1/2 teaspoon vanilla extract
- Zest of one large orange
- Slivered almonds, for garnish (optional)

Now that we have our ingredients ready, let's start baking! Preheat your oven to 350°F (175°C), and grease a 9-inch (23 cm) round cake pan.

Prep time: 20 minutes, Cook time: 40-45 minutes, Serves: 8

"The time has come!", as the walrus would say, to start mixing and baking. This cake is not only simple to make but also a true crowd-pleaser! The sweet orange and nutty almond flavors come together so perfectly that everyone will be begging for a slice (or two!).

Begin by whisking together the eggs and sugar in a large bowl until the mixture is light and frothy. Next, add in the orange juice, olive oil, almond flour, baking powder, baking soda, salt, vanilla extract, and orange zest, and mix until well combined.

Pour the batter into the prepared cake pan, smooth the top with a spatula, and sprinkle slivered almonds on top, if desired. Bake for 40-45 minutes, or until a toothpick inserted into the center of the cake comes out clean. Let the cake cool for 5 minutes in the pan, then remove it and let it cool completely on a wire rack.

An interesting fact about this cake is that in ancient Greece, they believed that the orange symbolized good luck and happiness. And who wouldn't want some good luck and happiness in their lives, right? So, go ahead and give this cake a try, and let the good luck and happiness flow!

And now, for the moment you've been waiting for - the nutritional values of this delicious cake per serving:

Calories: 385

Fat: 26g

Saturated Fat: 3g

Cholesterol: 68mg

Sodium: 259mg

Carbohydrates: 35g

Fiber: 2g

Sugar: 27g

Protein: 6g.

So, there you have it - a cake that's not only delicious but also nutritious! The perfect way to indulge in a sweet treat and feel good about it. Baking this cake is a win-win situation, if you ask me!

95. Figs and Honey Tart

Ladies and Gentlemen, welcome to the world of Tarts! Today we are making something super sweet and gooey, yet sophisticated and elegant. I'm talking about none other than the delicious Figs and Honey Tart. A perfect blend of flavors that will make your taste buds go wild. Ready to get baking? Let's do it!

Before we dive into the ingredients, let me ask you a question - Have you ever heard of a dish that requires only 4 ingredients and still tastes like a million bucks? Well, hold on to your hats because that's exactly what we have here. Just 4 simple ingredients that when combined create magic in your mouth! Here's what you'll need:

- Puff Pastry Sheets - 2
- Fresh Figs - 8
- Honey - 3 tablespoons
- Almonds - 1/2 cup (sliced)

Cooking this delicious tart will take about 25 minutes, with a total preparation time of 45 minutes, including making the pastry.

This Figs and Honey Tart is perfect for 8 people, or 4 people who want seconds...or thirds...or fourths...You get the picture!

Let's start with the pastry. Take out the puff pastry sheets from the freezer and let them sit at room temperature for about 10 minutes. Preheat the oven to 200°C (400°F). Roll out each puff pastry sheet on a floured surface to a 9-inch (23cm) round. Use a fork to prick the center of each round a few times.

Next up, the figs. Slice the figs into thin slices and arrange them in a circular pattern over the center of each pastry round, leaving about 1 inch (2.5cm) border around the edges. Drizzle some honey over the figs, and then sprinkle the sliced almonds on top.

Bake the tarts in the oven for about 25 minutes or until the pastry is golden brown and the figs are caramelized. Take the tarts out of the oven and let them cool for 5 minutes.

Serve warm with a scoop of vanilla ice cream or some whipped cream, if you like.

Once, I made this tart for a dinner party, and it was a hit! My friends couldn't stop raving about it. One of them even said, "This is the best tart I've ever had! It's like biting into a piece of heaven!" That was the biggest compliment I've ever received for my baking, and I still smile every time I think about it.

Per serving, this Figs and Honey Tart contains approximately:

Energy: 280 calories	Cholesterol: 0mg	Dietary Fiber: 2g
Total Fat: 16g	Sodium: 140mg	Total Sugar: 20g
Saturated Fat: 4g	Total Carbohydrates: 34g	Protein: 4g

And there you have it, folks! A delicious and nutritious Figs and Honey Tart that's sure to become a favorite in your home. Enjoy!

96. Almond and Lemon Semolina Cake

Oh boy, you're in for a treat with this Almond and Lemon Semolina Cake recipe! It's the perfect balance of sweet, tangy, and nutty flavors that will tantalize your taste buds and leave you wanting more. Are you ready to put your baking skills to the test and whip up a dessert that'll have everyone talking? Let's do this!

For the ingredients, we have:

- 1 cup semolina flour
- 1 cup almond flour
- 1 cup granulated sugar
- 1/2 cup olive oil
- 4 large eggs
- 1/2 cup freshly squeezed lemon juice
- 1 teaspoon baking powder
- Zest of 2 lemons
- Pinch of salt

Alright, let's get baking! This cake takes about 50 minutes to cook in the oven at 350°F. The preparation time is about 20 minutes, and it serves 8 to 10 people. Just enough for everyone to have a taste, but not too much to make you feel guilty.

Now, let's get to the fun part - the instructions! Start by mixing together the semolina flour, almond flour, and baking powder in a large mixing bowl. In a separate bowl, whisk together the olive oil, eggs, lemon juice, lemon zest, and salt. Gradually pour the wet ingredients into the dry ingredients and stir until well combined.

Next, pour the batter into a 9-inch cake pan and smooth out the top. Bake in the oven for about 50 minutes or until a toothpick inserted into the center comes out clean. Once it's done, let it cool for about 10 minutes before removing it from the pan.

An anecdote to share - I once made this cake for a friend's birthday and they were so impressed with the flavor and texture, they asked for the recipe on the spot! It's that good.

And finally, the nutritional information per serving (assuming 8 servings):

Calories: 405	Cholesterol: 87mg	Fiber: 2g
Fat: 23g	Sodium: 73mg	Sugar: 25g
Saturated Fat: 3g	Carbohydrates: 44g	Protein: 8g

So, there you have it, folks! A delicious and simple Almond and Lemon Semolina Cake recipe that's sure to impress. Time to preheat that oven and let's get started!

97. Date and Walnut Baklava Rolls

Ladies and Gentlemen, grab your aprons and prepare yourselves for a wild and delicious ride, as we're about to embark on a journey to the land of sweet delight, where a symphony of flavors collide to create a dessert that will tickle your taste buds, and make you want to dance in joy - the Date and Walnut Baklava Rolls!

Now, let's gather the troops and see what we need to make this flavor explosion happen. We'll be needing the following ingredients:

- 1 cup of chopped pitted dates
- 1 cup of chopped walnuts
- 1/2 tsp of cinnamon
- 1/4 tsp of nutmeg
- 1/2 cup of honey
- 1/2 cup of water
- 1 tsp of lemon juice
- 1 package of phyllo pastry (about 18 sheets)
- 1/2 cup of melted unsalted butter

So, you're probably wondering why we have such a diverse group of ingredients. Well, let me tell you, the dates, walnuts and spices form the filling that will make your taste buds sing, while the honey, water and lemon juice create a sticky, sweet syrup that will leave you wanting more. Finally, the phyllo pastry and melted butter are the icing on the cake, no pun intended, as they will create a crunchy, flaky crust that will make your mouth water just thinking about it.

Now, the time has come to put all the ingredients together. The preparation time for this masterpiece is about 20 minutes, while the cooking time will take you about 25 minutes. Trust me, it's worth the wait, as the end result will serve about 8-10 people, or maybe just you if you can't resist the temptation.

So, let's get to work! First, let's make the filling by mixing the chopped dates, walnuts, cinnamon, nutmeg, and lemon juice in a bowl. Next, in a saucepan, let's bring the honey, water, and lemon juice to a boil, then let it simmer until it thickens. Now, let's get our hands dirty and assemble the rolls. Take a sheet of phyllo pastry, brush it with melted butter, then place a spoonful of the filling at the end. Roll it up like a burrito, then place it in a baking dish. Repeat this process until you have used up all the ingredients. Finally, let's brush the top with the remaining melted butter and bake the rolls for 25 minutes until golden brown.

Now, let's talk about an anecdote. I remember the first time I made these baklava rolls, I was so excited that I ate the entire batch before anyone else could try them. I felt terrible, but also incredibly happy and satisfied. From that day on, I always make sure to share them with my loved ones, so they can experience the same joy I did.

Now, let's talk about the nutritional values:

Calories: 300 per serving

Carbohydrates: 32g per serving

Protein: 4g per serving

Fat: 20g per serving

Sodium: 80mg per serving

And there you have it, folks, a dessert that will make you feel like you're in a fairy tale, surrounded by sweetness and happiness. So, go ahead, make a batch today, and share it with those you love, and if you're feeling brave, try to resist the temptation to eat the entire batch like I did. Happy baking!

98. Chilled Honeydew and Mint Soup

Get ready to beat the heat with a delicious and refreshing Chilled Honeydew and Mint Soup. Imagine sipping a bowl of sweet honeydew and minty goodness on a hot summer day. This dish is the epitome of summer in a bowl and will keep you feeling cool and refreshed.

Here's what you'll need to make this chilled delight. But don't take my word for it, grab a pen and write these down, it's going to be a wild ride!

- 1 large honeydew melon (peeled and seeded)
- 1 cup fresh mint leaves
- 2 tbsp lemon juice
- 1 cup Greek yogurt
- 1 tsp honey
- Salt and pepper to taste

You'll need around 20 minutes to prepare this dish, including cutting up the melon, juicing the lemon and plucking the mint leaves. But once it's all prepped, you can sit back and relax for about 15 minutes while it's blending away to perfection.

Servings: This recipe will make about 4-6 servings, so feel free to invite a few friends over or save some for later.

Step 1: Take a large bowl and place the peeled and seeded honeydew melon, fresh mint leaves, lemon juice, Greek yogurt, honey, salt, and pepper in it.

Step 2: Now it's time to blend! Take a blender or food processor and blend the ingredients together until smooth.

Step 3: Pour the mixture into a bowl and chill in the refrigerator for at least 15 minutes.

Step 4: Serve the Chilled Honeydew and Mint Soup in bowls and garnish with mint leaves or lemon wedges. Enjoy!

Once, while making this soup, I added a whole jalapeño pepper instead of just a pinch of black pepper. The result was a delicious but spicy soup that had my guests reaching for the nearest glass of water. So, always double check your ingredients before you start cooking!

Here's a list of what you'll be fueling your body with in each serving:

Calories: 138	Sodium: 48mg	Sugar: 18g
Total Fat: 3g	Total Carbohydrates: 24g	Protein: 7g
Cholesterol: 6mg	Dietary Fiber: 2g	

99. Cinnamon Roasted Apples

Looking for a warm, cozy and comforting dessert to enjoy on a crisp autumn night? Look no further than Cinnamon Roasted Apples! These juicy, sweet and aromatic apples are the perfect addition to your dessert menu. They are easy to make, taste delicious and are also healthy. With just a handful of simple ingredients and a little bit of love, you'll have a tasty treat in no time!

Let's talk about the ingredients you'll need to make this delightful dessert. To make this delicious treat, you'll need the following ingredients:

- 4 medium-sized apples
- 3 tablespoons of unsalted butter
- 1/4 cup of granulated sugar
- 1 teaspoon of cinnamon
- 1/4 teaspoon of nutmeg
- a pinch of salt

The key to making this dish is to use the freshest, juiciest apples you can find!

The cooking time for this scrumptious dessert is 30 minutes. This includes preparation time and baking time. It's the perfect amount of time to enjoy a warm, comforting treat and it's ready just in time for dessert.

In terms of preparation time, you'll need about 10 minutes to get all the ingredients together and ready for cooking. This is a quick and easy recipe, which is great for busy nights when you want to enjoy a sweet treat, but don't want to spend hours in the kitchen.

This recipe makes 4 servings, so it's perfect for a small gathering or for a family dessert.

Now let's dive into how to make this delectable dessert. First, preheat your oven to 375°F. Then, peel and core the apples, slicing them into 1/4 inch thick slices. In a saucepan, melt the butter and add the sugar, cinnamon, nutmeg and salt, stirring until the sugar is dissolved. Add the apples to the saucepan and coat them with the mixture. Transfer the apples to a baking dish and bake for 30 minutes, or until they're golden brown and tender.

This recipe has been passed down through generations in my family and is a staple dessert for the autumn season. Every time I make this dish, I feel like I'm enveloped in a warm, comforting hug. And every time I take a bite, I'm transported back to my childhood, sitting in my grandmother's kitchen, surrounded by the sweet, warm scent of cinnamon and apples.

This dessert is not only delicious, but it's also healthy! Here's a list of the nutritional values for one serving:

Calories: 250

Cholesterol: 40 mg

Fiber: 3 g

Fat: 15 g

Sodium: 75 mg

Sugar: 26 g

Saturated Fat: 9 g

Carbohydrates: 33 g

Protein: 1 g

100. Cinnamon Roasted Apples

Once upon a time, in a magical kingdom of sweets, there was a dessert called "Turkish Delight". It was loved by everyone for its soft and chewy texture and the heavenly combination of sugar, nuts and rosewater. And today, we're gonna make this fairy tale come true in your very own kitchen!

Are you ready to gather your ingredients? Here we go!

For the Turkish Delight, you'll need:

- 1 cup granulated sugar
- 1 cup cornstarch
- 1 cup water
- 2 tablespoons lemon juice
- 1/4 cup chopped pistachios
- 2 tablespoons rosewater
- Red food coloring (optional)

Now, let's talk about the cooking and preparation time. This dreamy dessert takes approximately 45 minutes to cook and another 1 hour to set. It yields around 20 pieces of Turkish Delight.

Here's how you can make it:

In a large saucepan, mix the sugar, cornstarch, water, and lemon juice. Stir continuously over medium heat until the mixture thickens and starts to pull away from the sides of the pan. This usually takes around 20-25 minutes. Then add in the chopped pistachios, rosewater and a few drops of red food coloring (if using) and stir for another 5 minutes.

Pour the mixture into a lightly greased 8x8 inch square pan and let it cool completely. Once it's set, cut it into small squares and roll each piece in powdered sugar.

Anecdote: Legend has it that Turkish Delight was served to the Sultan in a palace made entirely of sweets, with fountains flowing with syrup and jewels made of jelly. And now, you can enjoy this royal treat right in the comfort of your home.

Nutritional Information (per serving, based on 20 servings):

Calories: 87   Sodium: 5mg   Protein: 1g

Fat: 1.5g   Carbohydrates: 21g

And there you have it! Your very own homemade Turkish Delight with Pistachios and Rosewater. A dessert fit for a Sultan!

Conclusion

And there you have it, folks! A delightful journey through the vibrant and aromatic flavors of the Mediterranean cuisine. From the sweet and nutty baklava rolls to the refreshing honeydew and mint soup, each recipe is a true celebration of the region's rich culinary heritage.

Now, it's time for you to put your culinary skills to the test and whip up one of these delicious dishes in your own kitchen. And, if you happen to be a foodie at heart, we would be thrilled if you would share your experience by leaving a review on Amazon. Your feedback is important to us and helps us improve our recipes for future readers. So, grab your apron, preheat your oven, and get ready to tantalize your taste buds with the flavors of the Mediterranean. Happy cooking!

Made in the USA
Coppell, TX
01 March 2023